Basketball Post Play

**Pete Newell
and
Tom Newell**

MASTERS PRESS

A Division of Howards W. Sams & Company

Published by Masters Press (A Division of Howard W. Sams & Co.)
2647 Waterfront Pkwy. E. Drive, Suite 300
Indianapolis, IN 46214

Published 1995
Printed in the United States of America

10 9 8 7 6 5 4 3 2

Library of Congress Cataloging-in-Publication Data

Newell, Pete.
    Basketball's post play / Pete Newell and Tom Newell.
        p.   cm.
    ISBN 1-57028-030-4 (trade pbk.)
    1. Basketball --Offense. I. Newell, Tom, 1947-   . II. Title.

GV889.N49   1995   95-18764
796.323--dc20   CIP

TABLE OF CONTENTS

ACKNOWLEDGEMENTS

We would like to thank the players featured in the photos of this book: former NBA Center and Big Man's Camp student Blair Rasmussen, Mike Fallquist, Mason Helms, Jeff Knoll, Dave Masin and Matt Shreck.

We also wish to acknowledge Family First Productions, Inc. of Seattle, Washington and the outstanding photography by Harley Soltes of Seattle.

The facility for the photography was provided by the Mercer Island Basketball Team and their coach Ed Pepple.

Also, we wish to acknowledge Bob Kloppenberg of the NBA for his contributions to post play defense.

Credits:

Cover design by Phil Velikan
Cover photos © Frank Howard
Editorial assistance provided by Kim Heusel and Pat Brady
Photography assistance provided by Phil Velikan

FOREWORD

When I think about Pete Newell and basketball, the first thing that comes to mind is that no single person has been as active in basketball as long as Pete. He has been involved in the sport for 65 years at the player, coach and executive level in every phase of basketball. At 80 years old, Pete is still active conducting clinics throughout the United States and around the world. I can't imagine another person who has spoken to as many people about the game of basketball than Pete has during his lifetime.

My second thought is that no one in the history of basketball has made the kind of contribution that Pete has made. The only people that come close in comparison are Clair Bee and Henry Iba. Pete has always been accessible to coaches, young and old, at all levels of competition. It would be impossible to determine the number of coaches who have benefitted from Pete's basketball discussions. There have been so many, and they include men and women at every level of play from junior high school through the NBA.

Through the years, I have had the chance to visit with nearly everyone who has played a part in making basketball the game it is today. I know of no one who has the grasp of the game and its many facets as Pete. He understands the balance that is necessary between offense and defense, and comprehends better than anyone else involved in basketball the fundamentals of offensive play equally as well as those for defensive play.

One of Pete's greatest contributions, however, is his willingness to share his vast knowledge with everyone involved in basketball — both coaches and players — regardless of the level of competition. He has done an incredible job of developing players, and not just the ones who played for him. Just as Ted Williams, one of the greatest baseball hitters of all time, was willing to help players on other teams, Pete has worked with players from many teams other than his own because he wants to see kids be the best they can be.

Pete's big man camps are recognized as the best developmental camps in basketball. Countless players have improved their games because of Pete Newell's interest. No one I know has kept abreast of the developments in the game in individual technique and team play as well as Pete. He is as knowledgeable about the game played today as he is about the game played before and after World War II. I get a genuine thrill every time I listen to Pete Newell's enthusiasm as he discusses basketball. I get the same feeling whenever I watch him working with kids, whether it's a spontaneous reaction on his part or during organized sessions at his camps.

As a college coach, Pete accomplished everything possible for a coach to achieve with his team. He was the first to coach teams that won NIT, NCAA and Olympic championships. His efforts have been rewarded with every award possible for a coach culminating with his induction into the National Basketball Hall of Fame. His philosophy and ideas through his final year of coaching at the University of California in 1960 have formed the foundation of virtually every successful college basketball program ever since.

Pete Newell brought defense to the forefront with the use of both half- and full-court pressure and combined those ideas with helpside defensive principles that had long been advocated by Henry Iba. His emphasis on shot selection at the offensive end has been incorporated into every successful offense for the past 35 years. His ideas are so widely used that many coaches today may be completely unaware that the concepts they are using can be traced back to Pete Newell and his coaching strategies at San Francisco, Michigan State and California.

But in final analysis, the number of championships a coach wins or the individual honors bestowed on him because of the play of his teams does not determine a coach's legacy. It's determined by what that coach has given of himself to the game of basketball. The great coaches who were truly involved with basketball's development — Henry Iba, Clair Bee, Joe Lapchick, Everett Dean, Nat Holman, Red Auerbach — gave much more to the game than they ever received from it. I believe I have studied the history of this game as well as anyone. Without hesitation, I put Pete Newell at the top of this list of great coaches and contributors to basketball.

Pete's major motivation in his 65-year career has been what he can do for the game and those in it, both players and coaches; never what the game could do for him. Pete Newell has been my friend and teacher for 27 years. I have not met a person whom I admire and respect more than Pete. Quite simply, Pete Newell is the best there ever was.

Bob Knight
Head Men's Basketball Coach
Indiana University

INTRODUCTION

The Basketball Coach

The basketball coach is a composite of many contradictory attributes. He is a motivator, yet at times a tyrant. He is charged with having the patience and understanding of a priest, but at times must take the posture of a dictator. In a game that generates unprecedented excitement and emotion, the coach is expected to control his emotions even when positioned within a few feet of the on-court action. This control is challenged regularly by officials who must make quick judgments on fouls or rules violations. Working under these conditions is but one problem facing a basketball coach.

The coaching profession has changed dramatically in the past 60 years. Before the mid-1920s, basketball coaching duties often were assigned to assistant football coaches in many of the largest and most prestigious collegiate conferences. Some teams were coached by volunteers or physical education faculty members. One of the Big Ten schools had 18 coaches in 21 years. The lure of basketball had not yet been felt by the public or the media.

By the late-1920s, however, basketball coaching became a profession. Legendary Kansas coach Phog Allen, along with Nate Holman, a former coach at City College of New York, worked with other colleagues in forming the National Association of Basketball Coaches (NABC). The association was instrumental in elevating the position of basketball coach from a delegated chore that was often reluctantly accepted to a professional position. As the NABC recognized basketball's growing popularity and the public's acceptance of the National Invitation Tournament, the NCAA tournament was organized.

During the 1930s, two important rule changes had a dramatic impact on basketball. The elimination of the center jump after each basket or free throw created a game that had a constant flow of action and a pace it had never before enjoyed. The other change was the institution of the center line, often called the 10-second line because the offensive team must bring the ball across the line from the backcourt within 10 seconds.

Because these rules were made just before World War II, it wasn't until after the war that their full impact was felt. And it was during this time that basketball began its greatest rise in popularity.

Along with basketball's growth in popularity came increasing importance and prestige for the NCAA tournament, fueling the growth in popularity among the general public as well as college alumni and high school associations. This growth would not have happened without the unselfish efforts of the coaches who volunteered their teams and conferences to experiment with new rules that have guided the direction of basketball from the inception of the NABC to the present.

Penalty or Foul

Basketball is a game of delicate balance. Maintaining a balance between the value of the ball and penalty of the foul is but one instance of the necessity for carefully monitoring the game annually. Only by continued input from the rules committees and guidance of coaches will basketball continue to thrive on the national scene.

An example of this balance can be found in the development of the three-point basket. Before the three-point shot was introduced, coaches rated players primarily on their inside abilities. Outside shooting skills, although noteworthy, were not a priority. That changed when the three-point shot became permanent. It also has helped United States players catch up to European and Asian teams who had come to rely on perimeter shooting because of physical size and the nature of international rules.

The current three-point line, however, causes an imbalance between the value of the ball and the penalty of the foul. Hitting one-third of the shots behind the three-point line is equal to making half of the shots taken inside the three-point line. In most instances, improvement in outside shooting from beyond the three-point line is greater than one-third. At the Division I college level it is closer to 35 percent. However, few teams now or in the past have consistently hit more than 50 percent of their shots from two-point range. A result has been fouling for profit by the trailing team in the final minutes of a game because the value of the one-and-one free throw opportunity does not have the percentage value of the three-point shot. The rules committee was wise to introduce the 10-foul penalty which gives a team two free throws after the opposing team has committed 10 team fouls in a half.

Outside shooting will only continue to improve, increasing the emphasis placed on perimeter shooting. Because of this, the three-point line, currently 19 feet, 9 inches for play through the college level, should be moved back to the international distance of 20 feet, 6 inches. This would improve the balance between the value of the ball and the penalty of the foul.

The Pressure of Coaching

There is no level of coaching today that can escape the pressures of the job whether they be the exterior pressures or self-imposed (interior) pressures. The interior pressures seem to be the same at all levels, but the exterior pressures may be greatest in the high-profile Division I men's and women's programs.

The exterior pressures have risen right along with basketball's growth in popularity that is equal to baseball and football. This growth has brought increased media attention throughout the country. Print media devotes more coverage than ever before to basketball, and television exposure has risen to levels that have far surpassed all expectations. Radio coverage, especially the call-in shows, has also risen dramatically.

I have seen this rise in popularity first hand. The NCAA tournament now ranks with the World Series and Super Bowl as a major event. But in the 1950s, I was charged with trying to sell the Final Four games to a network radio. There was no interest of any kind. Today, the Final Four is covered by every media company nationally and internationally. A ticket to the event is termed the hardest to buy among any of the major events.

Along with the growing popularity and prestige of basketball and the NCAA tournament, the demands on coaches have also increased. Not too long ago, a coach who won more games than he or she lost, did not feel threatened. Today, the barometer of successful coaching seems to be an appearance in the various NCAA or other postseason tournaments. The demand for tournament qualification is greatest at the Division I level because of the financial bonanza for the participating teams, but it also is present to a lesser degree at all levels of college competition.

Vast amounts of income are generated by radio, TV and ticket revenues at the Division I level. The money generated by the basketball and football programs not only helps support those programs but also the other sports that produce little or no income of their own. To encourage television coverage, the basketball coach is faced with the pressures of creating an attractive basketball program that will draw the fans both on TV and in person to new arenas, and satisfy alumni and students who seem only happy if the team qualifies for postseason play. Local media often demand not only a winning team but a dominant winner.

As great as these exterior pressures have become for some coaches, the inner, self-imposed pressures are shared by coaches at all levels. All coaches have a desire for their teams to play well. All coaches share the anxieties caused by the possibilities of team mistakes or individual breakdowns. All coaches worry about the unexpected.

"Have I prepared as thoroughly as I should have?" "Did I underestimate the opponent in any area?" These are some of the devils that dance in a coach's mind before a game. These mental images are not confined to the high-profile coaches. They are shared at all levels. A coach coaches to win, conscious at all times that the team may not be prepared as well as possible in certain areas, and hoping that the opposing coach fails to recognize those shortfalls.

When dealing with the obligations of the position, a coach should try to acquire a philosophical understanding of his or her profession and its inimitable pressures. The coach must disregard outside criticism from fans, media, alumni and the administration unless it can be seen as constructive criticism. A coach can always improve and must be critical of himself or herself in areas that may need criticism. This same open mind will recognize changes in the game that will require changes and adjustments in coaching and teaching styles as well as relationships with the players. One of the greatest challenges facing the coach has come away from the court where personal grooming and dress have changed dramatically. Too much rigidity in this area can create problems but a complete disregard for any form of a standardized dress code can be even worse. In the end, the coach must arrive at a standard with which he or she is comfortable and be consistent in seeing that it is followed.

Coaching — Teaching

The responsibilities of a basketball coach can be broken down into two categories — teaching and coaching. Some coaches are better teachers while others are better coaches. Still others are strong in both areas. The important thing is that a coach recognize the difference between these two responsibilities.

Coaching relates to the team and the many facets involved in developing a strong team concept:

• Conditioning factors related to team preparation.

• Development of a practice plan that deals with every area of team play and preparation.

• Development of an offense that can cope with any opponent's defense.

• Development of a defense that is best suited to the playing and coaching personnel.

• Refinement of both the offense and defense.

Because coaching pertains to a team, the coaches must be concerned with methods to motivate the team to give its best effort. And they must be aware that these methods change. When their team is favored to win a game, the coaches must prepare positive statements as well as tell the team how it will win the game. When the team is not favored to win, the coaches must sell the players on the great opportunity they have to upset the opponent.

But preparing a team to win isn't a coach's only job. He must prepare the players to properly react to many emotional factors such as hostile crowds, unfavorable officiating and discipline on and off the court.

Teaching relates to the individual plan of the players as it relates to offense and defense. As a "part-method" teaching approach proponent, I strongly believe in this area of a coach's responsibilities. Teaching addresses the players' individual needs.

Basketball is a game of countermoves and must be taught with an eye to explaining what the defense is taking away and what countermoves are effective against this defense. A teacher explains not only the "how" of this theory but also the "why." The "why" is the most important aspect of teaching basketball.

The teaching extends to two players helping each other create high-percentage shots by emphasizing the seemingly small details necessary for development of the shot — setting a proper screen and a fake by the ball handler that allows a legal, tight screen to be set. The teacher then blends three players, coordinating their efforts to create the shot with proper spacing, cutting, screening and passing. The teaching then extends to four players until finally, the fundamentals are ingrained in the minds of all five players by developing drills that relate as close as possible to the offensive strategy. When conducting these drills, attention must be given not only to the offensive execution by each individual, but also the defensive play. As the teacher builds the drills from one-on-one to five-on-five it's especially important for the defensive demands to increase with each level.

Once the teacher has prepared the individuals, the coaching takes over. The coach explains the component parts of offensive play so that the players understand the proper team concepts. On defense, they must be able to defend not only the player with the ball, but be ready to help a teammate who is guarding the player with the ball. Offense can be broken down into two-man, three-man or even one-on-one isolation games. But playing defense properly and successfully requires participation by all five players — not four, three or two, and certainly not by just one.

Despite its apparent complexities, basketball is really a simple game. Coaches have a tendency to overcoach and underteach but it's better to do a few things well than everything fair. Consistency is important to team success, but the road to achieving it begins at the coach's door — consistency in teaching, consistency in discipline, consistency in the approach to the players. What you do today you must live with tomorrow.

Pete Newell

Basketball
Post Play

This book is dedicated to Wayne Embry, the biggest of the big men.

HISTORY OF POST PLAY

In basketball's evolution and progression, tall players did not play an important role and were largely bypassed in the game's early days. The tall player was thought to be ungainly, poorly coordinated, slow in movement and lacking in physical strength. Coaches desired the more agile, quick and athletic types because basketball was a game of constant movement. The slower, less agile players were not favorably considered for play. There were few tall players of note before the 1930s, even though control of the center jump was the single most important factor of the game.

Basketball was, is and — I believe — always will be dictated by the rules committee. Historically, major changes in play have come about because of major changes in the rules. As the big player began to emerge, the rules affecting the area around the basket kept changing to minimize his effectiveness. The paint area at the offensive end of the court was known as the "key" when the three-second rule was enacted (1932-33). At its inception, the key was 6 feet across with a circle around the foul line giving it the appearance of a keyhole. As the game progressed, the key became wider and wider because the abilities of the big players dominated the basket area. It reached its current 12-foot width in 1956-57. The changes were designed to lessen the impact of big players who were less effective 12 to 15 feet from the basket. The NBA has since widened its paint area to 16 feet.

Some early big players of note were "Stretch" Murphy of Purdue, Harry Boykoff of St. Johns, and Carl Lubin, famous for his play on the 1936 Olympic Team. However, it was not until George Mikan of DePaul University and Bob Kurland of Oklahoma A&M that big players really gained national acceptance for their presence on the court. Both Mikan and Kurland were close to 6 feet, 10 inches tall. Both players towered over opponents and their teams' offenses were built around them. The period of their dominance started at the beginning of World War II (1941). Their individual success and the success of their teams caused many coaches to make the center the focal point in their offensive schemes. Post play and its development began during this period and continued to be a very important part of coaches' offensive thinking until the mid-60s.

THE EARLY DEVELOPMENT OF MOTION OFFENSE

As stated earlier, the rules committee is the real innovator in basketball. A change in the committee's interpretation of a legal offensive screen created a ripple that became a tidal wave. John Bunn, principle voice of the rules committee, redefined what constituted a legal screen. For many years, what was known as the 3-foot rule formed the basis for interpretation of the rule. Simply, the screener must stop at least 3 feet from the defensive player. Theoretically, this gave the defense one step to proceed around the screener as he followed his or her assigned opponent. If contact occurred within 3 feet from where the screen was being set, it was an offensive foul. Contact that resulted when a screen was set three or more feet away was a defensive foul.

This was an easy call for the officials to make, and it was not really a problem for the coaches at the time of the change. Many coaches never understood Bunn's reason for changing it, but change it did. This was the birth of motion offense, or the passing game as it is sometimes called. Although variations of the passing game were used sparsely in the 1930s, the motion offense allowed a screener to position himself against the defensive player in a manner that gave the defensive player little room for movement. The 3-foot rule was extinct as contact between screener and defensive player became a common occurrence with little blame assessed. If blame was assessed by the referees, it was usually against the defense.

Motion offense completely changed the theory of developing spacing and the shots on offense. To take advantage of the new offense, coaches had to space players in the vicinity of the "point" or three-second area. The use of motion offense developed the shot from the basket to a point approximately 15 feet from the basket; which, in turn, created a massing of defensive players in the basket area because the offense called for its inside players to be stationed in this vicinity. Because of the number of players in the paint area, backdoor action, weakside slices to the basket and cutters off the post player were less frequently used. Also, the change in the interpretation of the charge-block rule created a hazardous situation for a player driving to the basket off a dribble. The charge foul became a popular call by the officials. Many coaches taught their players how to effectively take a charge so the dribble drive to the basket became almost extinct. Coach Bob Knight took motion offense to new heights in the 70s and 80s and his success created popularity not only nationally, but internationally. It is still the most popular offense used today.

In motion offense, the center, or post player must effectively and aggressively screen off the ball to create an open shot for a teammate. A response to a switching tactic is a seal by the center or screener on the player he screens. Following the seal, the center pivots and moves toward the passer for the reception in the vicinity of the basket. The screens that make this offense effective are down screens. All of these screens are off or away from the ball.

In the NBA screens on the ball are the more widely used. The techniques are slightly different as the action is not often bothered by a collapsing weakside defense.

SPACING

Spacing is probably the most important facet of offensive team play. There is a distinct difference in spacing in the motion offense and spacing in a post offense, often recognized as a triangle set. In the motion offense, the spacing is in the basket area. By using downscreens, shooters emerge from the basket area to a shooting position 14 to 16 feet from the basket. Their teammates' downscreens give them the help to break free for the shot. In this type of offense, shots are created when the player comes away from the basket "off the ball."

In a post offense, the spacing requires the offense to extend from sideline to sideline trying to unmass the defense. Shots are created by weakside cuts and slices to the basket, backdoor moves, drives off the dribble or one-on-one play at the center position. Because the spacing is much wider if the defense tries to overextend in helping the defensive post player, the offense can counter with quick passes to the weakside offensive players or crosscourt skip passes from one sideline to the other.

The post player faces very different responsibilities in the two concepts. In the motion offense, the center is a screener and is usually effective in that role. He or she will also get into a receiving position after the screen for a quick post-up move which usually results in a jump shot near the basket. This player is usually not expected to make the same kinds of passes as a post-up center. He or she is usually not the focal point of the offense. Because of the crowded paint area, the hook shot, reverse drives and power moves are not especially popular shots because they can result in offensive fouls.

The post-up center does some screening but usually in the two-player game — a center screen on the ball. This player normally operates on the ball or strong side but sometimes moves to the weak side. When receiving the ball, the player must quickly read the situation. Is there a one-on-one situation? How does the defensive player match up? Is the defense overplaying the wing players making the backdoor pass a possibility? Is there double-team pressure? If so, who and where is the open player?

Because the defense is dispersed by the wide spacing of the forwards and guards, the center often has room to step out for a hook as the defense crowds around the paint area. Patrick Ewing and Ralph Sampson are examples of this point. Some "experts" predicted that Ewing would not be a scorer in the NBA because all he had was a fall-away turnaround jump shot. The same was true of Sampson, who also became a turnaround jump shooter. Ewing has a total post game now because the NBA rules against zone defenses lessen the chance for convergence on the post player by the defense. It was not the fault of their college coaches that they were not utilized in this way because the spacing changes that the motion offense brought into basketball were the catalysts for change.

As stated earlier, rules and interpretations dictate the play of basketball. The NBA, with its no-zone rule, makes the offense much more predictable. But in college and high school, the various zone and matchup defenses create many more problems for the offense. The post-up type centers in the NBA are similar in their development of offensive moves, passing skills, and their ability to read and react to situations to the pre-motion offensive post players. This transition of the big player's role when moving from college to the NBA created a need for my Big Man's Camp.

Another major rule change impacting basketball at every level was the addition of the three-point basket. The three-point shot, probably the most important rule adopted since the elimination of the center jump after each made basket, created major changes both offensively and defensively, and has caused coaches everywhere to reevaluate the skills his or her team needs to excel at its level of competition. The NBA now puts more emphasis on the range and accuracy of its guards and small forwards some high schools and colleges stress the importance of jumping ability and inside strength. Prior to the three-point rule, coaches often were heard to say, "If I'm going to be beaten, it will be over my defense, not inside of it." The three-point shot changed this type of thinking.

It is more than a coincidence that the NBA has never enjoyed the number of outstanding centers it does now. Three-point shooting has forced colleges to put more emphasis on sideline-to-sideline defense resulting in a change in some offensive thinking as more formations for the post player are being used. Some coaches intersperse their motion offense with some post-type, set formation or "sets" as they are often called. The three-point shot will eventually bring more creativity to high school and college offenses as their programs develop better outside shooters and more inside moves.

Because the NBA game is more predictable due to its no-zone rule, coaches have developed a variety of defensive maneuvers that comply with the rule yet prevent the offense from fully using the skills of the center. These defensive plays are simply a "doubling" of the post player by a second defensive player. The second defensive player is usually a defensive guard, but creative coaches change the doubler and bring a forward to double-team the post player. Offensively, countermeasures to this strategy are being fully exploited.

Symbols Used in Our Diagrams

Offensive Players: **1, 2, 3, 4, 5**

Defensive Players: **X1, X2, X3, X4, X5**

Player with the Ball: **(1)**   (Player's number is circled)

Path of Player without the Ball: ——————————→

Path and Direction of the Pass: — — — — — — — — →

Optional Pass: — — — —O— — — →

Path and Direction of Player
   Dribbling the Ball: VVVVVVVV→

Player Screening and Then Cutting: ———————⊢↘

Entry Pass: — — — — — — — — →

Player Cutting and Pivoting: —————————↰

Player Setting a Screen: ——————————⊣

PHYSICAL SKILLS

PHYSICAL SKILLS NEEDED TO BE AN EFFECTIVE POST PLAYER

There are many skills needed to make the most of your playing time as a post player. The most important are as follow:

HANDS

Strong, sure hands are a necessary attribute to be fully effective as a center. Often, when the center receives a pass in the traffic around the basket, a slight tip of the pass or a jostling opponent demands a reception of the pass. A dropped pass usually results in a loss of possession. Finally, in offensive and defensive rebounding, strong hands are a necessity in protecting the rebound.

These pictures accurately depict the importance of having good, strong, sure hands while playing against the various defenses trying to slap at the ball.

Rebounding with strong hands and protecting the ball is also a necessity.

POSITION OF THE ARMS

Most fumbles by an offensive center are usually attributed to "bad hands." This is often a misstatement, however. When the center's arms are pointed downward or carried at the side, the receptor resists the ball rather than recepting it, causing the receiver to be accused of having "board hands," a term used to describe a poor receiver. The position of the arms extended at chest level allows a center to "receive" the ball. In short, the hands should be bringing the ball to the chest level rather than resisting the ball. The post player should always keep his or her arms at chest level or higher to make it difficult for a smaller defensive player to touch the ball.

POSITION OF THE FEET AND LOWER BODY

Basketball is a game of quickness, balance and lateral movement. If a basketball player plays every minute in a college (40) or NBA (48) game, he normally has the ball in his hands less than $4^1/_2$ minutes. Yet that same player must use his feet throughout the entire game. Foot positioning skills are often the most identifiable traits of outstanding basketball players. An

These two pictures demonstrate the proper position of arms upon reception of the ball.

axiom of the game is that the ball is shot with the hands but "the quality of the shot will depend upon the feet." Creating a shot on or off the ball is directly related to the player's foot skills.

The accepted fundamental stance is a flexed knee position with a wide but comfortable foot position, arms up and extended toward the ball. This low-based stance will counter the physical defensive pressure a post player often receives from opponents when coming to meet a pass. After the reception, the ball should not be brought to the body but held 12 to 18 inches from the chest. The hips act as a swivel as he protects the ball from the outstretched arms of the defensive player. This same low-to-the-floor stance enables the post player to "seal" or fence-off the defensive player trying to deflect a post pass. An upright position by a post player should never be tolerated by the coaches. A high stance can easily be moved and directed by an aggressive and physical defensive player.

Basketball is a game of habit. Sometimes the habits are bad; sometimes they are good. A habit is a conditioned reflex created by repetition. Because we naturally stand in an upright position, this habit spills over to our

POSITION OF THE FEET AND LOWER BODY

1

2

3

4

Observe the flexed knees and wide base position of the feet by the offensive post players in pictures 1 through 4. The ball is away from the body (chest) allowing the post player to make any pivot move with the ball. Note in pictures 3 and 4 that the smaller post player is able to properly seal the defender by utilizing the low-to-the-floor stance.

basketball players. Playing basketball properly requires a flexed-knee stance both offensively and defensively. All motion usually commences when the knees are flexed. If a player stands straight up with stiff knees, the flexed-knee opponent has a clear advantage in any movement reaction. In short, the player goes from stiff knee to flex knee and is repeatedly beaten because he is one movement behind.

FOOTWORK

The importance of fundamental footwork and foot skills is never more evidenced than by the fact that a player handles the ball roughly 10% of the game yet plays 100% of the time with his feet. It matters little if a player is well above average as a shooter if he doesn't have the foot skills to create a shot on or off the ball. Every phase of basketball —defense, screening and rebounding — demand fundamental footwork.

The great majority of players have a master eye, a natural arm and one foot they are more comfortable using than the other. In short, we are right- or left-handed, right-eyed or left-eyed and right-footed or left-footed. Although most players try to increase the strength of their weaker hands, far too few players realize the importance of developing equal ability in both feet.

The offensive elements of basketball are shooting, passing, dribbling, screening and offensive rebounding. In each element, footwork and foot skills are extremely important.

SHOOTING

Without a good balance of weight on each foot and the proper lift of the legs, consistency of shooting will not be achieved. When a player takes a jump shot off the dribble going right or left, good footwork will eliminate the "float" some shooters develop due to a lack of abilty to lead with either foot. A simple lay up requires the proper lift of the foot as the player takes off into the air. Hook shots by post up players demand the proper steps to effect a smooth and fluid shot.

DRIBBLING

The individual skills of the feet are best evidenced in the art of dribbling. Most coaches, when addressing fellow coaches at the various clinics held

annually, advocate that an offensive driver will beat the defensive opponent on the first step or he (or she) won't beat the defensive player at all.
Players who have not developed their left foot (or their least natural foot)
will normally take a short step initially and depend on their natural foot,
usually the right, to attempt to successfully beat the opponent. The opponent is seldom defeated if the first step is not a long step. In this instance
the need to develop the weaker foot is of paramount importance if the
player is to be a threat in either direction. At my Big Man's Camp each day
we change sides of the court. When developing foot fundamentals and
individual skills, we establish the inside foot as the pivot foot. If the right
foot is the pivot foot, the players must step off with their left foot. When
shooting or dribbling a basketball with the weaker hand, a player will
eventually gain confidence in his weak hand and achieve the ability to
play with either hand. It is the same with the feet. By forcing the players to
use their less-natural foot, soon a long step with their left foot will become
natural to them and the players will present a much more effective offense
to the defense.

The individual skills of a dribble can make an offensive player rise to
another level as the defense tries to copy with their skills.

PASSING

Body control and balance are essentials of fundamental passing. Many
passes are made while in motion but body control must be maintained if
the offensive player wants to avoid turnovers. Some players have the bad
habit of leaving the floor with their feet and committing themselves in the
direction of the pass. Often interceptions are the result of these telegraphed
passes. With good foot balance and control, a pass can be faked or delivered. It can be changed from a chest pass to a bounce pass should the
need arise. Balance begins with the feet so the footwork of a player has its
importance in passing.

SCREENS

Good reflective screens and good footwork are synonymous. To effectively screen, the screener must have a low base with the feet comfortably
spaced and balanced so that the screener can turn and become an immediate offensive threat.

There are various types of screens. Down screens are an important phase
of motion offense. The use of a back screen can compound the problem a
defensive player faces if the defensive communication is poor. Side screens
are a big part of an effective two-man game and are probably the most
used of all screens in the NBA. Regardless of the type screen used, it is
important that the screener set a low base that he or she is able to hold
when the screen encounters the physical contact of the players that are

screened. The screener should be positioned as close to the defensive player that is being screened as legally possible. Further, the ballhandler should always fake away from the direction of the teammate who is screening.

It is an axiom of basketball that the better a player screens, the better the chance of a good close shot for the screener. Simply, a strong close-up screen often causes the defense to switch. When a switch by the defense is effected the screener has an advantageous position on the player he has screened. By the use of a low base and a rear pivot, the screener has sealed his opponent and is in a very good position to receive a pass with the defender behind him. If there is no switch, the offensive player using the screen has an open and unopposed shot.

The screener should always use a low base with the ability to rear pivot in either direction as he seals his opponent. Whether the screen is on the ball or off the ball the fundamentals don't change.

A basketball player plays half the time on the court on defense. Quickness of movement both covering the player he is guarding on the ball and covering the opponent off the ball requires quick initiation of movement. The flexed knees stance and position are necessary to assist the feet in maintaining proper fundamental defensive position. Ball denial by an alert, moving defensive player makes defensively playing the opponent when he gets the ball much easier. Denial forces ball reception farther from the basket.

I have always employed a drill that demands foot movement. Too many players overuse their hands on defense and in so doing lose the good low balance necessary. It is less difficult to defend if you reach, but it is less effective. My drill for this fundamental is that the defensive player playing a wing man with the ball is only allowed to use his feet and never permitted to reach with his hands. Good individual defense in positioning between the ball handler and the basket is paramount — and good positioning begins with the feet.

REBOUNDING

As described in the rebounding chapter, a good low base is an essential in defensive rebounding. Offensive rebounding is alertness, anticipation, immediate movement and foot faking to create a problem for the defensive rebounder in a screening position. For both offensive and defensive rebounding, good foot skills are essential. This skills are covered in depth in pages 93 to 94.

PASSING

DEVELOPING CORRECT POST AND/OR CENTER PASSING

One of the differences between the centers of today and those in basketball's early years is the lack of ability by today's players to make the right pass at the right time.

A number of centers in the past excelled in this phase of the game. Three that prominently come to mind are Wilt Chamberlain, Wes Unseld and Bill Walton. Another, Kareem Abdul-Jabbar, was also a superior passer especially in his ability to hit the cutters going to the basket. This skill is no longer as prominent in the NBA as it once was. Although there are some fine passers, motion offenses are not conducive to the development of a variety of passes for centers to make.

Chamberlain and Walton could execute any pass. Unseld and Walton were superior outlet passers enabling them to initiate the fast break with quick and accurate outlet passes both long and short. They were often able to make the pass while in the air or as they secured the rebound giving their teammates a number of advantages as they quickened the ball on their fast break.

Chamberlain was able to make any pass and held every NBA passing record a center could hold. Because of his great height, Chamberlain had a better view of a cutter to the basket than a normal sized center of 6 feet, 10 inches. He had a great touch and a great sense of how and when to throw the proper pass. Abdul-Jabbar was the consummate offensive center. His great intelligence enabled him to make passing a major part of his total game.

Great passing skills in a center are an art form that the game today sadly lacks. Today's centers usually don't receive the early instruction in their position as did the centers of earlier generations. Many of today's coaches have never been exposed to the post-up type cutting game making it difficult for them to teach or embrace the offense's intricacies.

A center is called upon to make a variety of passes, but the most common needed from the post are the bounce pass, the overhead one-handed or two-handed pass, the baseball pass, the fast-break outlet pass or the overhead pass.

THE BOUNCE PASS

The bounce pass is a situation pass. It is an effective pass when thrown to a receiver cutting to the basket. Basically, it is a slow pass as its trajectory is not direct, and it is not effective when passed to a receiver standing still or adjacent to the ball handler. However, it's ideal when trying to hit a moving receiver. The receiver will be able to see the ball easily and pick it up as it hits the floor in most instances. And because the bounce pass is low to the floor, a defensive player seldom deflects or touches the ball. Since the bounce will slow the ball's velocity, however, it's important for the passer to lead his teammate a greater distance than he would when making a chest or other similar pass.

Close-up of free-throw line extended

To best explain or describe a bounce pass by a post player, you might say it is a fundamental pass thrown out of congestion for a cutter going hard to the basket. Remember that a bounce pass to a cutting receiver will often eliminate the extra dribble leading to a layup. If the pass is led correctly, the rhythm of the play is continuous. The receiver will not have to gather his balance as he would with a jump or stride stop, and can continue with the easy play to the basket.

The bounce pass must be practiced. It should have a slight overspin, but it must never reverse spin. Only with practice will the center be able to gauge the proper distance between himself and the cutter. When properly used, the bounce pass is an effective counter measure against defenses that depend on double-teaming the opposing center. Also, a retreating defensive player is at his or her weakest when the bounce pass is used.

THE FAST BREAK OUTLET PASS

The fast break outlet pass is not easily mastered. It's thrown from a very crowded area — the basket area after a defensive rebound. Both Bill Walton and Wes Unseld had great ability to rebound the ball, turn in the air and deliver the ball to their outlet receivers. Unseld, in particular, could accurately throw 60 to 70 feet to a streaking teammate from out of rebounding traffic. It was an exceptional gift as he was less than 6 feet 8 inches tall. Walton could rebound, turn and overhead a two-handed pass before he touched the floor. Like Walton, Unseld also used a two-handed overhead pass.

To be a great outlet passer, a center must first be a great rebounder. Wilt Chamberlain's rebound statistics are phenomenal when compared with the numbers of today's leading rebounders. Chamberlain delivered the ball to his receivers using a baseball-type pass that was quick and accurate. He could hit receivers on the run 60 to 70 feet away.

The overhead two-handed pass must be practiced to be properly executed. Too often, easy basket opportunities are lost because the outlet pass loses trajectory and falls short of its intended target like a felled duck. The overhead two-handed pass can be deflected and often jarred loose if the post player holds it too long in the crowded area under the basket.

The baseball pass must be thrown with a break of the wrist and hand inward. This will insure the trajectory needed for the pass to reach its target — usually a receiver breaking away from the pass. If the wrist goes outward, the ball tends to assume the same downward trajectory or momentum as a curveball thrown by a baseball pitcher. This pass demands a level path, not a downward path, as it picks up velocity. However, as most players are not able to palm a basketball and make an accurate baseball pass, I recommend focusing on the two-handed outlet pass.

CENTER MOVE HIGH POST BACK DOOR BOUNCE PASS

This play is a "read and react" center move. Notice that the wing player releases when the guard has picked up his dribble to initiate the pass to the wing (top). The wing receiver then steps toward the passer as he knows the center's read on this defensive pressure is to release to the high post, free throw line extended (bottom). (Action sequence continues on facmg page.)

CENTER MOVE HIGH POST BACK DOOR
BOUNCE PASS (CONTINUED)

Upon reception of the ball, the center establishes a wide base with his footwork (bottom, previous page) so as to better drop-step-seal the opposing center and also to make the proper bounce pass to his teammate on a back door or back cut play (top). This is an excellent 3-on-3 practice drill for both ends of court. Flip-flop the sides every four or five times. This drill allows the head coach to oversee both ends while the assistants direct action.

OUTLET PASS FROM A DEFENSIVE REBOUND

Here you observe the defensive center rebounding the ball after blocking out. He pivots with the knees flexed for balance (upper right) to make a two-handed outlet pass to the guard (lower right). It is very important to remember how the center pivoted with the defender on his back (upper right) and that this motion has caused the defender to lose his balance and step back (upper left and lower right), creating a clear passing lane to the outlet receiver. Remember that the center never brought down the ball below his head. He protects the ball by having both hands on the ball for a solid follow-through (lower right) overhead outlet pass.

THE OVERHEAD PASS

There are sound reasons for centers to know when and how to use the overhead pass.

- Because it is normally in the view of the receiver, it is usually caught.
- It is held high, decreasing the chances the ball will be jarred loose by smaller players.
- It is a quick, easily delivered pass to an outlet as a "fan" pass.
- It can easily be faked to open a passing lane.
- The overhead pass is often more accurate and can be thrown a much longer distance than a chest pass.

The fundamentals of the overhead pass are to hold the ball at its axis and quickly flip the wrist. The hands and wrist should break outward upon release of the ball.

OVERHEAD PASS FROM POST POSITION

In this sequence, the wing passes to the post-up center. Observe how the center has a target hand for the passer to read (left). As the center receives the ball, he is closely guarded by the defensive center and also the wing passer's man (right). (Action sequence continues on next page.)

OVERHEAD PASS FROM POST POSITION (CONTINUED)

Notice in the photo in the upper left that the offensive center always keeps the ball high above his head and extended away from the outstretched arms of the double down defense. The offensive center reads the defense quickly, looking to see if the point is open also (upper left). It is important to look as some teams will rotate over to an open wing player on kick-out passes. The offensive center recognizes quickly there is no rotation, and he passes back out to the wing player for open shot (lower left). Notice how the kick-out pass is made with both hands on the ball and that there is perfect extension and follow-through on the pass.

ANOTHER SCENARIO FROM THE DOUBLE DOWN COMING FROM THE TOP DEFENSIVE GUARD

The pass is again from the wing. The double down is from the top guard; the offensive center looks out front (left). The offensive center waits for rotation on defense (right). Keeping the ball above his head, the center then kicks out to the open man on top for a shot or drive. Note how the offensive center pivots to make a balanced kick-out pass using both hands.

5

THE HOOK SHOT

SHOOTING: THE EARLY HISTORY OF THE HOOK SHOT AND ITS DEVELOPMENT

Basketball in its earliest stages had no frame of experience to guide it. The ball was large and had no pebble for gripping it. Few players could palm the ball, and if anyone dunked it, it was a well kept secret. The basic shots that evolved from these initial stages of development were the two-handed set shot and the hook shot. Because there were no references to speak of, both shots were shot in a variety of ways, especially the two-handed set. The hook shot was a popular shot by all players as it was made while in motion and it had a certain flare to it that players liked. Gradually, as the ball was improved, the hook shot became identified as a post player or center shot.

In the development of the hook shot as a real threat to a defense, it had its detractors. The big man as center for a variety of reasons has had to overcome a number of obstacles. In the early stages the tall player was often bypassed by coaches because their agility and speed were considered to be sub-par. Prior to World War II, the "fan shaped" backboard was introduced. Soon it was adopted by some high school associations as the only legal backboard. Hook shots did not deflect from all wooden backboards the same, so the center often had to adjust his target point on the wood. The fan shaped board caused real problems to many hook shooters, as it was not board but a tinny type of metal and it was not rectangular like the wooden board at that time and our present glass boards. In early 1942 I was stationed at Great Lakes and was a member of their base basketball team. One of the greatest college hook shooters of that time was George Glamack, a North Carolina All-American. His hook shot was a high angled shot off the corner of the rectagular board with a sharp spin that caused it to angle sharply to the basket. Because George had glasses that were as thick as the bottom of a Coca-Cola bottle, his was a "feel" hook. We could turn out the lights and George would still angle that hook through the basket. One night, in the arena where the fan shaped board was born, we played our opponent on a court with the fan shaped board. Glamack's first three shots were what we would now call air balls. That upper part of the rectangular board was missing on the fan shape. After the third airball George just walked over to the bench and sat down without anything but a murmur that termites had really eaten that board. We played no more games with the fan shaped board.

The first center that really gave attention to the hook shot was George Mikan of De Paul and later the great NBA champions, the Minnesota Lakers. Ray Meyer, a young coach of the time and a Hall of Famer now, took this gangly awkward 6'10" youngster and diagrammed exactly where he wanted him to play on offense. It was an area about six to eight feet on each side of the basket and less than 10 feet in front. Coach Meyer and George spent countless hours over George's college career learning the fundamentals and with repetition, George soon acquired a fluid hook shot both to the right and the left. Mikan is still considered at that highest plateau where our great centers have earned their place. Some players of lesser size like Cliff Hagan, an All American at Kentucky and a member of the NBA champion St. Louis Hawks, used the hook shot as their main weapon in their arsenal of shots. This shot has been successfully used by players other than those over seven feet.

The hook shot was taken to its highest art form by Kareem Abdul-Jabbar. Probably no shot or shooter has, as yet, been introduced that could rival Kareem's sky hook. The fluid, sweeping grace of Kareem as he stepped to commence the sky hook has been remembered by anyone who had the good fortune to see this marvelous athlete perform. To this day, I have never understood why young tall players have not been coached to develop this shot. Some say the dunk is the preferential shot of today's players, but how many players can dunk a basketball today in the basket area without getting it blocked? Conversely, a hook shot over the basket area congestion is seldom blocked. Bernard King, a 6'6" small forward was renowned for his great offensive game. His "baby hook" as we termed it was successfully arched over the heads of the shot blockers in his time.

In the present era of the game, the offensive responsibilities of the post up player have changed at the high school and college levels. The center is frequently a screener who is the second option in many instances. The spacing of these offensive sets is totally different from the NBA or post offensive sets. In the college offense the offensive shot is created with down screens or side screens in the basket area. The shot that is developed is usually moving away from the basket. The massing of the defense in the basket area gives the second option. The center has little space to shoot anything but a quick turnaround jumper. As I have explained, the rules and interpretation of the screen was the reason for this type of offense. In the NBA the no-zone rule and limitations placed on all off the ball defensive players created the post type game we have in the NBA today.

As veteran coaches retire, younger coaches who may not understand the proper mechanics of the basic hook shot may refrain from teaching it to avoid teaching it the wrong way. But remember this: the hook shot is one of the earliest and most basic shots in basketball. It can be banked off the glass (backboard) or attempted as a straight release shot without the bank.

Following is a description of the basic hook shot and its chief uses:

1. It is a wrist and finger shot. If delivered properly, with fingertip control and follow-through, it can be a soft, light ball on the glass. The mechanics are the same whether it is a right- or left-handed shot attempt.

2. When attempting a hook shot, the ball should be extended from the chin level. If a right hook is being attempted, the left hand is the guide hand and should not be released from the ball until the ball is about to be released. The left hand and arm should not be extended to push the defensive man away but kept high as the ball is being released. In this instance, the lead-off foot is the left foot and should be pointed toward the baseline. If the step-off is proper, the right hip will unlock and allow for a fluid follow-through. Conversely, if the step-off foot is pointed toward the side line, the hip stays locked and the result will be a disjointed shot or an off-balance attempt. Remember that the key element in this shooting mechanic is the leadoff foot toward the baseline, which allows for a proper instep pivot as the right hip unlocks, which in turn allows for a balanced, confident, high-percentage shot attempt.

As I mentioned before, possibly the greatest single shot associated with a player is the famous sky hook of Kareem Abdul-Jabbar. It was a right hook with a step to the baseline, shot with an extended arm, and a wrist and finger release nearly impossible to block.

But as great and effective as this shot was, it really didn't achieve recognition until Kareem complemented it with a left-handed shot in the opposite direction. When defenses began an extreme overplay to lessen the sky hook's effectiveness, Kareem answered with his left-handed shot in the opposite direction or toward the paint area. This serves as another example of the importance of countermeasures in response to overplay by the defense.

When countering the defensive post player who has overplayed the hook shot toward the baseline, the offensive post player steps to the middle of the paint area with the lead foot, in this instance the right foot, pointed toward the opposite sideline. This opens up the shooter's left hip for a fluid left hand hook.

THE BASIC HOOK SHOT

The play begins with the offensive center opposite the ball (see diagram on the next page) and creating the necessary space to receive the pass for his basic hook shot. In the top left photo the offensive center has both hands receiving the pass and seeing the ball into his reception. In the top right photo, the ball stays chin high, the knees are flexed and the eyes are focused on the basket (not the defender) as the center pivots with his inside foot toward the basket (bottom left) and continues the mechanics of the shot. He keeps his off hand in a flexed-arm positon (bottom right) as he goes up for the shot. (Action sequence continues on facing page.)

BASIC HOOK (CONTINUED)

The center does not push off or extend extend forearms (left) as he rises up to the fully extended top of his release form for his hook shot (right). Notice how accurate the center's release, follow-through and shot trajectory are toward the basket. Remember this move is only effective when the center has properly released to receive the pass. The center must keep the ball chin high, his knees flexed and his eyes on the basket as he goes into the basic hook shot mechanics. It is extremely important that the step-off foot of the center, as he steps toward the middle for his hook shot, has his toes of the step-off foot pointed toward the opposite sideline. This foot position allows for the unlocking of his right hip (in this above instance) this creates a fluid rhythmic hook shot.

Location of center's positioning to receive pass

OFFENSIVE POST PLAY

OFFENSIVE POST PLAY: BASIC MOVES

Centers must develop and be able to use many more shots than the other offensive players on a basketball team. The coupling of dribbling and footwork skills needed to become successful at the position is the foundation on which the great Hall of Fame centers built their careers. Centers who develop variety in their shooting present even more problems for their defensive opponents.

An offensive player must learn when and how to perform a shot. In a game of individual and team counters, the defense will try to take away an offensive strength so the offense must be able to read the overplay and effectively counter it. Each player must learn to read the defense and react to the weakness. Basketball is a game of read and react.

TURNAROUND JUMPER

Probably the most popular shot among centers is the turnaround jumper from 10 to 12 feet. This is the one shot a college center can shoot without committing an offensive foul or losing the ball in the congestion of the basket area. He can quickly release the ball before the converging defensive players can block or deflect the shot.

This shot can be even more effective if the shooter uses a pump fake to attempt to force a physical reaction from the defensive player. The fake will complement the turnaround or stationary face-up jump shot as an eager shot-blocking defensive player often only reacts to the shot possibility. Once the pump fake is used by the offensive center, the defensive player is less likely to react to the jump shot as quickly as he did at first because of the possibility of the fake. In baseball or softball, a pitcher with only a fastball is often hammered but when he can change speeds, the hitter can't be certain of the speed, making the fastball more difficult to hit.

TURNAROUND JUMP SHOT

In the photos above, the offensive center receives the pass at the medium post with the defender playing off (left). The placement of his ball reception allows the post player to take a turn-around jump shot (right). Keep in mind that if your post player catches the ball in the medium post area he has two options for shot selection: straight shot or bank shot (see photo on right for angle of the shot).

To make the pump fake effective, it's necessary to use the proper technique. In the upper torso fake, the knees stay in a flexed position and the ball is faked to a level of the head and not overfaked. If the knees become stiff or the ball is faked too high, it's ineffective.

COUNTERS

There are many counters that complement post-up hook shooters, particularly when the step-off is to the middle. When the post-up player has made several baskets with a step-off to the middle, the defensive post players often anticipate the shot and leave their feet in an attempt to block the shot.

UP-AND-UNDER

The counter to the overplay involves the post player taking a short dribble to the middle, thereby anchoring the step-off foot but being able to continue with the extended arm of the hook shot. Now the defensive opponent is caught off balance, and the post player continues with the extended shooting motion, stepping across the planted (or step-off) foot and proceeding to the basket by taking off from the second foot as it plants. The post player actually shoots the ball after the plant and leaps from the same side from where the movement began. It is called an up-and-under move and is very effective against a shot-blocking defensive player. But the technique of the fake shot, step across and the plant requires much practice. It is a specific counter against a particular type of defensive player or an eager shot blocker.

Another effective counter in a similar situation is the reverse drive from a move toward the middle. This move works against a defensive opponent who overplays the post-up player to the middle. Simply, it's a short dribble to the middle with a reverse step and takeoff upon completion of the reverse. It's not as difficult as the up-and-under move but very effective if overplayed to the middle.

THE SPIN MOVE

The spin move is very popular and extremely effective for a low-post player when aggressively played and leaned against by the defensive matchup. The mechanics of this counter demand the inside foot be the pivot foot — the foot nearest the baseline with the opposite foot describing a front turn that is completed by a turn facing the basket. It should be a long step as the post player takes the dribble to complete the turn and face the basket. The aggressiveness and direction of the defensive post player and his or her momentum causes the player to go in one direction (toward the post player in matchup situations) and the post player in the

UP-AND-UNDER COUNTER MOVE

1

2

3

The up-and-under counter move begins when the center receives a pass in the medium post (1). The center steps toward the baseline to draw the defense off balance (2), allowing the offensive center to turn pivot as if he is about to shoot a hook shot (3). (Action sequence continues on facing page.)

UP-AND-UNDER COUNTER MOVE (CONTINUED)

4   **5**

He must keep the ball above his head throughout the movement for full fake effectiveness. He then steps through the defender (4) and over with the ball for an easy layup (5). When you introduce this move, take your time. Develop sequences that allow players to gain new confidence with their footwork and balance. Don't put in a defender until the move has been practiced for two or three days. In this instance, the right foot is the pivot foot as the center fakes, executes a front turn and, after a shot fake, drives past the defensive man for a close-in shot.

Basketball Post Play

UP-AND-UNDER COUNTER MOVE AGAINST OVERPLAY BY THE DEFENSE

1

2

This is the similar to the up-and-under counter move, but it requires a different offensive recovery (3). (Action sequence continues on facing page.)

3

UP-AND-UNDER COUNTER MOVE AGAINST OVERPLAY BY THE DEFENSE (CONTINUED)

4   **5**

The unique footwork shown here allows the center to score an easy layup (4, 5). It should be noted that the short dribble into the point area enables the center to cause his step-off foot to become the pivot foot and this allows for the fake hook and step-through with his left foot as he goes under and up by the defensive man.

REVERSE PIVOT

1

2

3

The reverse pivot is also similar to the up-and-under counter move. The difference is that the defense has over-committed toward the ball fake (3, 4). (Action sequnce continues on facing page.)

REVERSE PIVOT (CONTINUED)

4

This allows the center to reverse pivot to the basket for an easy layup (5, 6).

5

6

SPIN MOVE

1

2

3

The spin move, a very quick and effective
post move, begins with the post receiver
seeing the ball into his hands (1). The
defensive center moves up and into the
post receiver with contact (2). The offensive center keeps the ball chest to chin high
away from his body and looks to the
middle to make the defender think that
the offensive center is going to turn into
the middle. The head fake makes the post
defender reach over the offensive center's
shoulder for the ball and shift all of his
weight to the lead foot, creating a momen-
tary imbalance from a defensive position.

SPIN MOVE (CONTINUED)

4

5

Correctly reading this play, the offensive center counters with a quick pivot-spin move off the foot closest to the basline (3, 4) which creates the space needed to get by the flat-footed defender and use a one-dribble move (5) to finish the play with an easy layup or power dunk shot (6). It is important to remember that the pivot-spin is made on the ball of the foot, not the heel. Pivoting on the heel is an off-balance skill that is difficult to overcome once learned. The ball should not be dribbled until the spin is completed and the center is facing the basket.

6

opposite direction (toward the basket) because of the front turn. This turn causes the defensive player to lose contact as the front turn leaves the defensive player pushing air. It's at its best against a physical, pushing, aggressive, intimidating type of defensive player.

A good post player must always recognize where the defensive opponent is playing. On the high side? Low or baseline side? Fronting the post players? Or is the defense playing behind and allowing an entry pass? Let's examine each position.

COUNTER MOVE ON THE HIGH SIDE

The defensive post player who plays on the high side when the ball is on the wing is vulnerable for a pass toward the baseline side. If the wing players try to pass to their post player from the wing or foul line extended, the angle of the pass poses little problem to the defense. But if this wing position improves the passing angle with a dribble toward the baseline, the passing angle can assure the post player of an close-in shot. The post player must seal or screen the defensive player and not release from the seal until the wing player completes the dribble. This insures timing and considerably reduces the chances of an interception or deflection. It is very important the post player holds the seal until the wing player picks up the dribble.

COUNTERS ON THE LOWSIDE DEFENSIVE PLAYER

When the defensive player is low or baseline side, the counters differ. The team defense attempts to help the defensive post player with a sagging defensive front line player. If the defensive post player doesn't get any help, however, a quick turn to the middle when the post-up center receives the ball usually creates a close-up shot in the paint.

The most effective counter when the post player is played on the low side begins with an entry pass from the free-throw line. When the ball is passed from the wing to the weakside offensive forward who comes to the foul line, the post-up player seals (screens) and keeps the opponent from establishing a defensive position in the paint. When the wing player makes the pass to the foul line, the offensive post-up player is in excellent position to receive the pass from the foul line if the screen has been maintained.

COUNTER MOVE WHEN THE POST PLAYER IS FRONTED

The most common counter is the lob pass by the wing over the fronting defensive player. It is very important that the post-up player not release from the fronting opponent until the pass is directly overhead. If the offensive center or post-up player releases too soon, the fronting defensive player can deflect or intercept the lob.

A drill that we do at our Big Player Camp to emphasize the importance of timing in the post-up release is have the offensive post player turn his back to the passer, look straight up at the ceiling and only release when the ball comes into view. Invariably, the pass is caught in the basket area with no difficulty reinforcing the point that proper timing makes the lob pass effective.

COUNTERS TO A DEFENSIVE CENTER WHO PLAYS BEHIND THE POST-UP PLAYER

Normally, this is a very weak defensive position, as a post player who has the ball six to ten feet from the basket invites an easy shot and more often than not a foul by the defensive player. A center who is an effective shot blocker will allow the pass and rely on the shot-blocking abilities. Also, when the defense double-teams the offensive center, the defensive post player will allow the pass. How the offensive post player counters against this type of defense is explained on pages 50 and 51.

THE OPEN SHOT FROM THE MEDIUM POST AREA

It is important for the post-up player to be seen as an offensive threat when facing the basket about 14 to 16 feet away. The defensive player will slough off and invite the shot. The slough-off lessens the effectiveness to pass inside or drive to the basket.

Some of the individual foot skills the post-up center will find useful are the shot fake and drive to the basket, explosion step move, a step back move, the pump fake and jump shot. David Robinson has added a very versatile face-up game to his back-to-the-basket post-up game and his points per game have increased dramatically as a result. A post-up player who can go outside has a real advantage because he or she can take a bigger, less mobile opponent outside and post up a smaller and physically weaker opponent.

COUNTER MOVE ON THE HIGH SIDE

The wing receives a pass from the point guard (1) and reads a 3/4 denial on the post-up center (2). The wing dribbles ball to the sideline one or two times to allow the center to seal his defensive man (3). (Action sequence continues on facing page.)

COUNTER MOVE ON THE HIGH SIDE (CONTINUED)

4

5

The wing executes a bounce pass to the post-up center (4), and the center makes an easy layup (5). The post up center must hold seal until the wing has picked up the ball upon completion of the dribble.

COUNTER TO POWER MOVE FROM THE BASELINE FROM HIGH SIDE DEFENSE

1

2

3

In this sequence we observe the post receiver catching the ball from the wing or point position. The defender commits his left foot defensively to stop any power move to the middle (1). Once the offensive post player has read the opponent's position, he makes the defender commit even more toward a power move to the middle by keeping the knees flexed for balance and looking toward his opponent and the basket (2). The offensive post player makes an above-the-head ball fake without lifting either foot (3). (Action sequence continues on following page.)

COUNTER TO POWER MOVE FROM THE BASELINE FROM HIGH SIDE DEFENSE (CONTINUED)

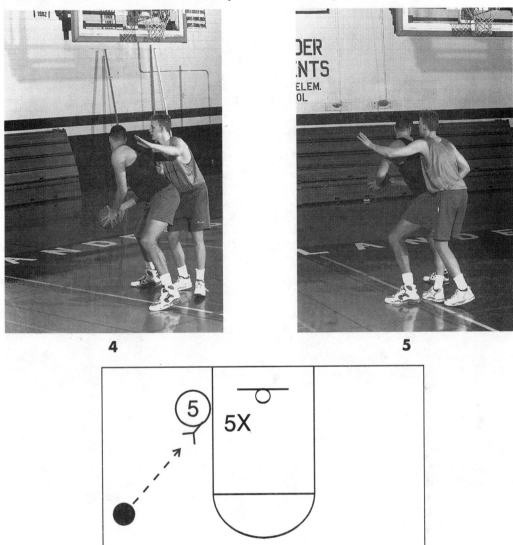

The offensive post player's ball fake forces the defender to overreact and lose his balance and position to recover and defend the baseline power move (4, 5). For this to be effective, the post player must keep his knees flexed, ball fake above his shoulders, and then move with a drop-step toward the baseline with contact to keep his opponent off balance for a shot. This is but another example of the importance of the jump stop for the post center when receiving the ball. The jump stop allows either foot to be the pivot foot. This creates real problems for the defensive man as the post up center can attack in either direction.

POWER MOVE TO THE MIDDLE —
COUNTER TO LOWSIDE DEFENSIVE PLAY

1   **2**

The offensive post player receives a pass from the wing player after coming to a jump stop with the feet parallel. He establishes his pivot foot only after reading the defender. Upon reception, the offensive post player reads the overplay denying the baseline power move and looks toward the defender and basket (1). The offensive player executes an above-the-head ball fake to further draw the defender closer and off balance (1). The head fake allows the offensive player to make a simple one-dribble power move to the middle with the knees flexed (2, 3). (The action sequence continues on facing page.)

POWER MOVE TO THE MIDDLE — COUNTER TO LOWSIDE DEFENSIVE PLAY (CONTINUED)

3

4

Notice that the offensive post player keeps his head up as he goes into the power move, keeping the defender on his heels when the post player dribbles to the basket (3,4). This play can finish with either a power dunk, layup or soft hook. Remember that the keys to making this play effective are reading the defender, countering with a move in the opposite direction once the defender is off balance with the ball fake, keeping the knees flexed and head up, and using one dribble (if needed) to finish the motion toward the basket. One of the best counters to a double down type defense is the power move quickly to the basket. The defensive post often moves toward the baseline side anticipating his help from the dribbling teammates who will cut off the post man's path to the middle. A quick offensive player will often beat the defense before it is positioned to take away the middle.

COUNTER MOVE VERSUS A FULL FRONT DEFENSIVE CENTER

1

2

The ball is located on the wing with the defensive center in a full front position (1). The offensive post player takes the blockout position with his head up (2). (Action sequence continues on facing page.)

COUNTER MOVE VERSUS A FULL FRONT DEFENSIVE CENTER (CONTINUED)

3

4

He holds this position until the pass is directly overhead (3) for the easy layup (4). It is important for the center to look up at the ceiling, keep his hands up and release only when the ball comes into sight.

THE OPEN-UP SHOT FROM THE MEDIUM POST AREA

1

2

3

This move begins when the offensive center receives the pass in the medium post area (1) and recognizes the contact hand in the back (2). He reads the defensive center's overplay to the baseline power move and then takes a hard step to the baseline with a ball fake (3). (Action sequence continues on facing page.)

THE OPEN-UP SHOT FROM THE MEDIUM POST AREA (CONTINUED)

4

5

The ball fake draws the defender completely off balance, and, after reading the defender properly, the offensive center reverse pivots to open up his position (4). The offensive center quickly goes into his shooting motion in the space created before the defender can recover to stop the open shot (5).

FACE-UP DRIVE TO THE BASKET

The offensive center receives the post pass with both hands on the ball (1). He executes a reverse pivot to face-up to the basket (2) with a shot fake to draw the defense off balance (3). The offensive center then drives to the basket for an easy layup. Don't over fake the ball as it enables the defense to recover and better defend this move.

POST PLAYER COUNTERS TO A DOUBLE-TEAMING DEFENSE

One of the most practiced counters to the talented scoring centers is the double-team. Sometimes it even becomes a triple-team. It follows a coaching axiom of not allowing the inside proficient scorer to beat you. The double-team is the invitation to pass the ball from the double-teamed center outside to an open perimeter player. With proper offensive spacing, the perimeter offensive players outnumber the opponents 4 to 3. Often, the double-teamed center is at a low post with the defensive player behind. The defense often allows the entry pass to the offensive post player and depends on the double-team to discourage an offensive move for a shot.

We are amazed at the consistency of the one response of so many offensive centers who dominate the ball, lose their shot opportunity and then hurriedly pass the ball out to the perimeter people. This is a counter to the double-team but certainly not the only counter, nor, I believe, the best counter. We will explain each counter I propose for the coaches who depend on the inside scoring of their talented post players.

Proper spacing can never be emphasized enough in an offensive scheme. Certainly not when it applies to an effective post-up player. However, different types of spacings are needed to counter the double-team. Perimeter standing is one of these. Movement or slicing to the basket is another type of spacing we believe is vastly underutilized by today's coaches.

MEDIUM POST OPEN-UP STEP BACK MOVE

1

2

3

4

The offensive center catches a pass mid-post from the wing position (1). He opens up to the defense by reverse pivoting on his right foot (2) which becomes his inside foot for the step-back move (3). Notice that the offensive center initiates his step to drive with his left foot toward the lane and the basket at the same time his begins dribbling (4, 5). (Action sequence continues on following page.)

MEDIUM POST OPEN-UP STEP BACK MOVE (CONTINUED)

5

6

7

8

The defensive center loses his balance on the step and dribble, which causes his weight to be on his outside left foot. The offensive center recognizes that his move has created the necessary space to pick up his dribble (all the while keeping the knees flexed) (6) and step back to his right (inside) foot for a square-up open jump shot (7, 8). It is important to notice that the offensive center keeps his head up as he goes into his motion and that the dribble is mid-body when released, not ahead of his foot. It is very important tht the offensive player steps toward the basket on the drive thus forcing the defensive man back. Upon the completion of the dribble, the step back must be back and out. This will create a good shooting base.

MOVEMENT OR SLICING SPACING COUNTER

In this counter, the offensive post player must move to a higher post position even though the opponent is playing behind him or her. Basically this post position is in the area of where the rebounder stands when a free throw is being shot. It was called the "nick" when the paint area and the foul line circle were called the keyhole. Moving the post to this higher position causes the opponent to move away from the immediate basket area.

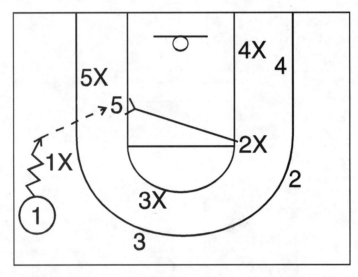

Diagram A

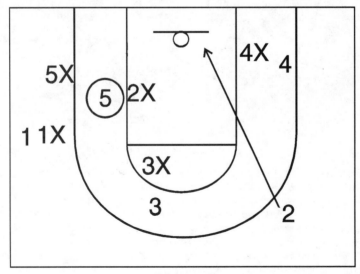

Diagram B

When player 1 passes the ball to the post player and the weakside X2 guard doubles the ball or the post player, player 2 immediately slices to the basket. The post player, upon receiving the ball, reads the double-team and looks to the weak side. He has a simple read of player 4X's defensive reaction. If 4X has not come into the paint area, the post player gives a bounce pass to his slicing guard, player 2. This pass should be angled slightly toward the basket so the offensive slicer can see the ball and be able to take it to the basket without a dribble. Should 4X recover quickly and be positioned to contest the shot, player 4 is alone within 12-15 feet of the basket for an open shot.

Should 4X immediately protect the basket when he sees the slicer (2) go the basket, the offensive post player 5 reads this overplay and pitches ball to the open player 4.

Simply, when the double-team comes from the off-defensive guard, it leaves only one defensive player to cover two players — 2 and 4.

This position at the high post gives the offensive post player proper angle and distances. The player becomes more of an offensive threat should the opponent try to protect the basket area by picking up the slicer 2. Reverse drives to the basket or a turnaround 12-foot shot are but two of the counter moves when 5X loosens up his defense to pick up the slicer. Sometimes the double comes from the passer's player, X1. If the post is on the strong side, the strongside forward 3 should make a backdoor cut and vacate the area, and player 1 should quickly move to the open area as 3X has had to vacate the area to defend the backdoor slicer 3. Should the double-team come from 4X, the post player 5 should pitch the ball to 4 who is slightly inside the foul line extended. Player 4 should space himself away from 2's opponent, so X2 is not in any position to hurry 4's shot. If 4 is a good leaper, a high lob in the basket area is also a counter if 4X leaves this position open.

When the single post offense was a very popular system, another axiom used by coaches emphasizing this type offense was, "Always look in the direction of their extra pressure. That's where the open player usually is." It's obvious the rotating player left the assigned matchup, and if the spacing is proper, this leaves an offensive player open. Rotation by the defense will sometimes counter this, but rotation is difficult in this situation, and regardless of the rotation, four offensive players cannot be closely guarded by three defensive players if the offense is spaced correctly.

THE LOW POST AND COUNTERS

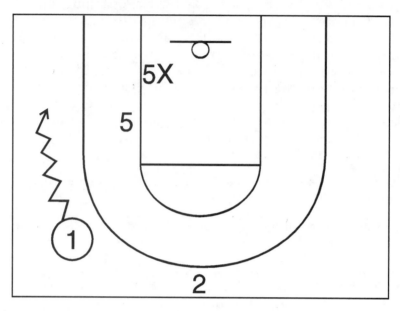

Diagram A

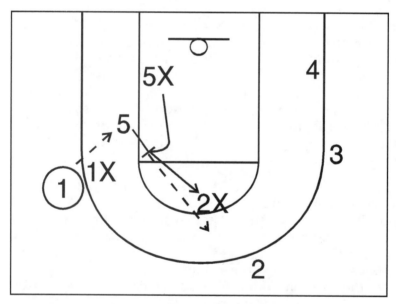

Diagram B

The low post is the most commonly used post position by teams today. When the double-team tactic is used by the defense, the defensive post player plays behind or at the side of the offensive post player, player 5. It's almost an invitation to throw the ball inside so the double-team will take place and encourage the post player to pitch the ball to the perimeter people.

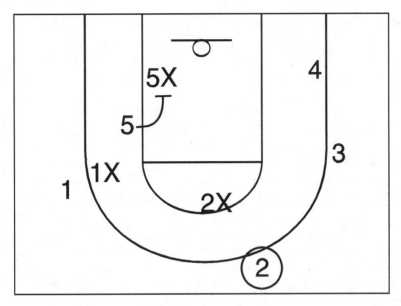

Diagram C

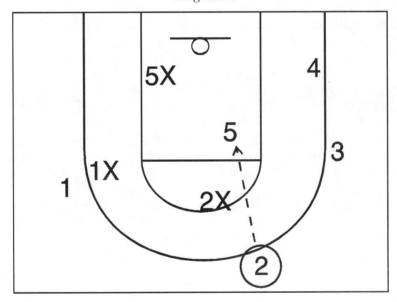

Diagram D

From this low-post position, 5 has poor angles and lengthened distances to the perimeter people. Slicers to the basket are no real threat in most instances because their reception of the ball is too close to the basket. Unless 5 dribbles away from the basket to create a little space for the slicer, the defensive post player, 5X, will reject most shots in the basket area.

Here are two of the best counters to the double-team in the low post.

1. An immediate, aggressive offensive move for the shot by player 5. If the defensive player plays behind the post or on the side, 1 can get the inside pass and move toward the unguarded side before the double-team player converges on them. It's usually a smaller opponent so the post player should hold the ball high while making a move, or dribble quickly and bring the ball to a high position when the ball is picked up. This offensive move must be done immediately as the double-team reduces the movement area of player 5.

2. When the post player, 5, is being doubled he immediately pitches to the open perimeter teammate. As soon as 5 pitches the ball outside, it's important for 5 to always seal (screen) the opponent and be in a receiving area for a return pass. The double-team defensive player is often caught trying to reverse the defensive path leaving the double-team to cover the open player usually leaving the matchup. Player 5 is open in the paint area for whatever shot is appropriate as 2 returns the pass to player 5.

These counters to the double-team defense are different in nature. Simply, a counter is an answer to an opponent's tactic or strategy. For an offense to be really effective, it's necessary to read these tactics and strategies and answer with tactics of your own. These counters are best taught in "part-method" teaching — breaking down offensive sets into component drills that are all segments of the five-player set. When offense is taught to players in a part-method manner, which is the intellectual or mental approach of "why," the coach is emphasizing a tactic that will make the player more effective as he or she continues to understand the reasons for counters and when to apply them. If a player can blend natural physical talents and skills with a mental understanding of why he or she reacts in a particular way, the result will be more effective and flexible play. The simplicity of basketball is best understood by players who have been exposed to part-method teaching. It means more work for the coaches but real success is seldom attained by teams and coaches without a work ethic. The price of success is sweat and the price of sweat is work!

Don't forget it.

CENTER SKILLS AWAY FROM THE BASKET

CENTER SCREENS ON THE BALL IN THE TWO-PLAYER GAME

One of the biggest difference between college and professional basketball is the types of screens used at each level. In the college game, most offenses depend on screens off the ball. The motion offense, flex offense and the "T", or triangle, offense are all basically built around off-the-ball screens, while most NBA offensive schemes revolve around on-the-ball screens. The 24-second shot clock is partially responsible for the NBA style since rules do not permit the weakside defense the same latitude allowed at the college level.

In the NBA, a defensive player must remain within a specified distance of his opponent or an illegal defense or no-zone rule is enforced. This allows the NBA to make better use of the two-player game which is usually the center setting a screen on a teammate's defender. Proper offensive spacing away from the ball lessens the help the two defensive players can depend upon for support.

One of the most difficult adjustments a college player must make if he reaches the NBA level is defending the two-player game. Few colleges play this type of basketball so the NBA rookie right out of college has probably never had to fight over a 280-pound center screen as he attempts to stay with his defensive assignment. It can be a difficult task even for the experienced NBA player. Some NBA coaches may use as many as eight defensive schemes to combat the screen on the ball in the two-player game. Basically, NBA defenses discourage switching except in prearranged situations. Being forced to switch assignments can create difficult mismatches for the defense.

In this chapter we explain center play away from the basket. It is important that centers develop the face-up game as well as the back-to-basket play. The same footskills forwards use to develop their facing shots are also practiced by the post player. The more a post player understands about forward play, the better his total game will be.

TWO-MAN PICK-AND-ROLL

The diagrams below illustrate the two-man pick-and-roll. The guard, No. 1, dribbles toward his defender, 1X, as the offensive center, 5, moves toward 1X to set a screen. 1 uses the screen to dribble to the left forcing 5's defender, 5X, into a switch to guard 1. This allows 5 to reverse pivot and break to the basket as 1 makes an easy pass that should result in a layup. (See the visual illustration on the following pages.)

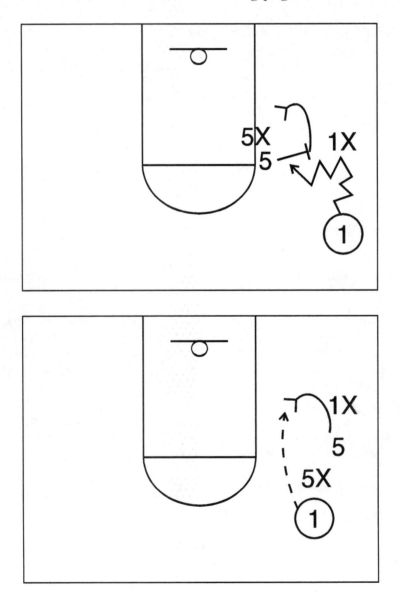

TWO-MAN PICK-AND-ROLL

1

2

3

Observe the wide-base screen set by the center (1). His arms are inside his waist so a foul for pushing cannot be whistled. After the guard with the ball uses the screen (2), the center opens up to the ball (3). (Action sequence continues on following page.)

TWO-MAN PICK-AND-ROLL (CONTINUED)

4

5

6

The center executes a reverse pivot (4). This forces a defensive switch (5) and creates a lead for an easy over-the-top pass to the center for a layup (6).

CATCH AND SQUARE UP

The catch and square up drill is a simple drill that emphasizes one of the most important facets of individual offensive play. When the offensive player advances toward a pass in the offensive end of the court, he should immediately attempt to face up to the basket with the ball positioned about chin level. With the offensive player looking at the basket with the ball positioned as described, he is in what has been termed the triple-threat position. From this position, the offensive player has three options — shoot, pass or dribble.

One of the most common mistakes players make is predetermining what they will do when they receive the ball. Good shot opportunities are often lost because the offensive player was thinking drive. Good passing situations are lost because the offensive player was thinking shot when there wasn't a shot available. A basketball player must first read the defense and then respond. Don't presuppose — read and react!

WING POSITION

At my Big Man Camp, the post players are involved in the mechanics of playing the wing X position. With few exceptions, centers or post players in the NBA are often asked to move outside 16 to 20 feet. This change of positioning by the post player creates an added dimension to his offensive game, and if respect is commanded from the defensive opponents, the middle will open up because of the attention given to the wing position of the center. Of the present highly regarded centers in the NBA, David Robinson of the San Antonio Spurs has developed a remarkably effective game facing the basket.

There are many reasons for developing offensive work at the wing area or at a distance of 16 feet from the basket. The distance should be at the limit of the player's effective range. The consistent encouragement and repetition each player experiences from this position as he or she gains confidence will present a new awareness towards footwork and the multiple footskill moves that accompany each practice session. This will also add a new dimension to the post-up player's back-to-the-basket moves.

The following footskill moves are what wing players will develop facing the basket.

1. The reverse step and drive versus overplay/lunge defense

2. The spin move versus closeout tight/contact defense

3. The reverse step and face up versus recovering defense but hands are down and there is no closeout on face up

4. The Kiki move (one dribble, step back) versus tight, forced baseline defense

Also included in this repertoire of offensive moves from the wing are the fake and speed drives to the basket in either direction, plus the rocker step and the two-dribble pull-up jumper along with the pump-fake drop-the-shoulder drive-to-the-basket move.

Every individual footskill movement is a counter to the defense that is being played. The confidence an offensive player achieves when answering a counter with his or her own patented move presents a difficult matchup for any defensive opponent. Furthermore, the offensive player's mental concepts of basketball broaden as he becomes more adept of the read and react motions. Thus the player becomes more of a student of the game and soon realizes how much more there is to learn and develop in his or her own game.

With this in mind, I include the fundamentals of wing play in my Big Man Camp drills. The footskills are similar in many instances to that of a back-to-the-basket post player. While few centers can effectively operate from 20 to 22 feet away from the basket, they may find success from an area 15 to 16 feet away.

INITIAL POSITION OF THE WING MAN

It is very important for the wing man to initially start from a low position. For example, should the advancing guard dribble the ball quickly upcourt and beat his defensive man, the wing man can easily clear the area of himself (A)and his defensive man. This opens up the side of the court for his teammate who has beaten his man and allows the guard to dribble drive to the basket (B).

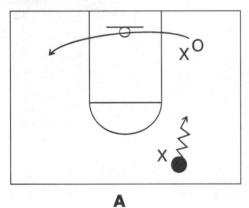

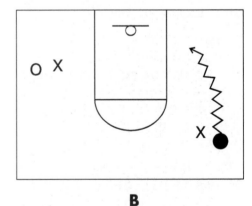

A   **B**

KICKOUT PASS VS. DOUBLETEAM FROM WING DEFENDER

1

2

3

4

This typical double down from the passer is very important for the offensive center to read and not predetermine too early. If the center takes the ball (2) and tries to effect a quick move without reading the defensive reaction to the post pass (3) there is a serious chance of a forced shot (rushed) or turnover (stripped ball, blocked shot) than if the center reacted correctly by kicking the ball out to the open man on the wing (4).

WING RELEASE, CATCH AND SQUARE UP
WITH THE INSIDE FOOT AS THE PIVOT FOOT

1   **2**   **3**

4   **5**

This play is also called the "turnout: catch and square up with the inside foot as the pivot foot." These pictures capture the correct positioning for ball reception. The player executes a jump stop with the feet parallel and the knees flexed (1). The ball is "seen" into the offensive center's hands and is kept in the triple-threat position (2). The offensive center reads the defense which is loose (3, 4, 5) and leaves the necessary spacing for the jump shot. The offensive center reacts to the defense by squaring up his inside foot as he pivots and begins movement into the jump shot (4, 5). (See diagrams on following page)

WING RELEASE, CATCH AND SQUARE UP
WITH THE INSIDE FOOT AS THE PIVOT FOOT

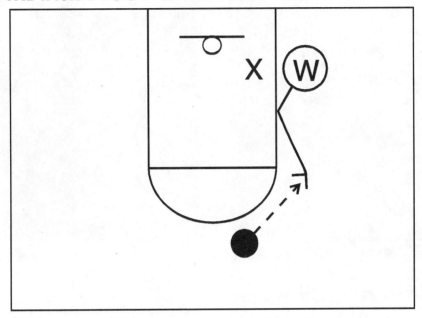

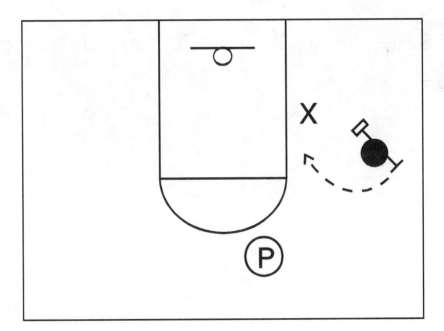

The wing receiver must step off with the right foot toward the ball and release to the wing with the left hand extended as a target. This will serve as a reminder for the receiver to come to a jump stop and pivot with the inside foot. It also will teach the passer and receiver to use non-verbals in the sequence of offensive play.

WING RELEASE SQUARE-UP JAB STEP WITH INSIDE FOOT AS THE PIVOT FOOT

In this sequence, the receiver is catching the ball on the wing and coming to a jump stop with the feet parallel to the point passer (1). In the first sequence, the offensive receiver reads the defender in two ways. The defender has his hands below the waist for defense on the ball that allows the offensive wing player to shoot, but the offensive player needs better spacing for a shot release (2). Recognizing the situation and keeping the ball in the triple-threat position, the offensive player takes one jab step toward the basket, creating a motion fake with his step that forces the defender to back on his foot closest to the basket (3). The defender's weight and balance shift and he loses position because the defender thinks his opponent is driving toward the basket, thereby creating the necessary space that the offensive player needs to create a square-up set shot or jump shot (4). Remember that a simple foot fake toward the basket always confuses a defender who closes out on the ball properly.

SHORT WING RELEASE BY CENTER
WITH FACE UP SHOT ON INSIDE PIVOT FOOT

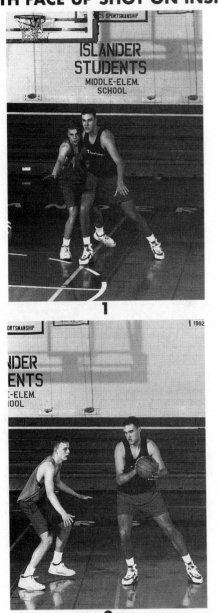

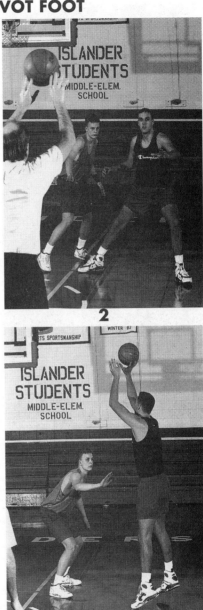

The offensive post player takes one step high toward the ball at the top of the key (1). Without pushing off with his inside arm against the denial defense, the offensive post player causes his opponent to lose his balance backward, thereby creating the lead for reception by the post player (2) and allowing him to receive the pass with both feet parallel to the passer (3). The offensive post player reads the loose defensive position by the defender (3), pivots on his right (inside pivot) foot and front turns into a jump shot (4).

WING RECEPTION WITH ONE-DRIBBLE STEP BACK

1

2

3

This is similar to the previous wing release sequence. The same principles of reception and footwork apply, but the difference is utilization of the one-dribble, step back, jump shot move that has become one of the most used one-on-one moves today. The read-and-react play of this move comes from the offensive player creating the necessary space to release a medium range (12 to 15 feet) jump shot. Notice that the defender is closer to the ball and the offensive player (1) than in the previous wing release sequence. The offensive player initiates the first step toward the basket with a dribble (2). It is very important that the dribble be put down in the middle of both feet with the off-hand protecting the ball in a flex elbow position (3, 4). (Action sequence continues on facing page.)

WING RECEPTION WITH ONE-DRIBBLE STEP BACK (CONTINUED)

4

5

The defender reacts to the foot and dribble motion because he thinks his opponent is driving to the basket (4). When the defender realizes his mistake and becomes off balance, there is nothing he can do but hope the shooter misses when he steps back (5) and releases his shot (6). Again, it is important that the step back is out as well as back. Photo five shows the proper shooting base.

6

CENTER LEAD WITH A DROP STEP DRIVE TO BASKET VERSUS AN OVERPLAY DEFENSE (RIGHT FOOT IS PIVOT FOOT)

1

2

3

The offensive post player creates a lead to receive the ball from the point. The defender reacts to the pass reception (2) by lunging and overplaying the position established by the offensive center (3). (Action sequence continues on facing page.)

CENTER LEAD WITH A DROP STEP DRIVE TO BASKET VERSUS AN OVERPLAY DEFENSE(CONTINUED)

4

5

The correct read-and-react play is executed by the center as he drop steps and reverse pivots with his left foot (3) and steps toward the basket, sealing the defender from recovery (4). He then makes the easy basket (5).

CENTER LEAD SHORT WING RELEASE WITH DROP STEP TO BASKET FOLLOWED BY SQUARE UP FOR SHOT

1

2

3

The center lead is similar to the two previous short wing releases. In this case the defender is not lunging or overplaying, but he is still close enough to eliminate the center lead/front turn jump shot (2) and not likely to drop-step the drive as in the previous center lead wing release drive (3, 4). (Action sequence continues on following page.)

CENTER LEAD SHORT WING RELEASE WITH DROP STEP TO BASKET FOLLOWED BY SQUARE UP FOR SHOT (CONTINUED)

4   **5**

The correct read-and-react play to this situation is to take advantage of the defender's off-balance position and the spacing created by the drop-step (4). The offensive center comes back squared up and goes into his shooting motion because the defender cannot recover in time (5).

Basketball Post Play

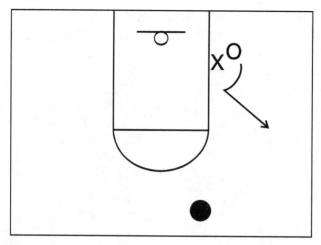

C. Execute reverse turn to pin defender and proceed to wing area to receive pass

Note: These release plays can be executed with three or four steps to initiate area of reception in operational zone.

The initial position of the wing player is midway between the sideline and the foul lane. It should be about 6 to 9 feet from the baseline. In this position, the wing player has four basic possibilities of movement which are all fundamentally sound. These movement possibilities follow:

1. The offensive man is low enough to create defensive problems for an aggressive, denying defensive man. His first move should be a fake to the middle with an attempt to get his inside leg across the legs of the defensive man. If he successfully does this, he seals his defensive man and angles to his proper spacing to receive the pass. The proper spacing is the court position best described as the foul line extended to approximately 5 feet from the sideline.

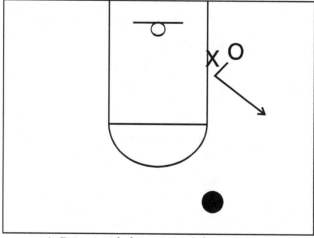

A. Drive inside leg across defensive man
B. Proceed to operational zone

2. Should the denying defensive man front the wing man, the wing man should fake toward the sideline and circle the defensive man from the foul line area to his normal spacing and receive the pass.

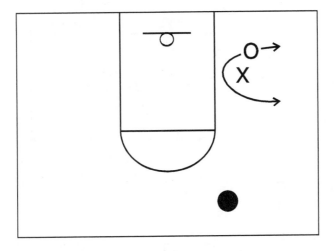

A. Fake one step toward the sideline
B. Circle to the inside of the defensive man
C. Cut to the operational zone

3. Often a fake of an extended arm by the wing man as he is deployed near the baseline is effective. The offensive man signals to the defender that a high pass is coming. As the defender turns his head to look for the ball, the wing man quickly darts to the foul line extended area and receives the pass.

4. By anchoring his inside foot, the offensive man begins four to five feet closer to the basket. Notice that the feet are parallel to the passer.

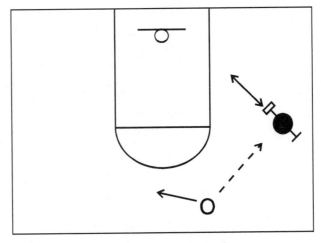

a. Inside foot as pivot foot

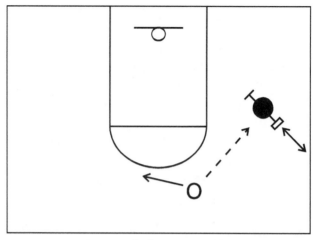

B. Outside foot as pivot foot

5. If the wing man moves in to a position closer to the foul lane area, he can screen the defensive guard as in the below diagram as he hands the ball off to a cutting teammate.

Each day, we change sides of the court, which means we change the pivot foot. This changing of the pivot foot also creates a habit of stepping off with either foot on a drive. Many right-handed players are limited when they go left because they have not developed their left foot.

Using the outside foot as the pivot foot can create a problem protecting the ball against a tight defense. The offensive player is denying himself a quick reverse turn and he has no foot fake to drive off his defensive man. He is 4 to 5 feet farther from the basket as he squares up and he can't help a circling teammate with an effective handoff.

THE BACKDOOR MOVE

The importance of timing between the passer (guard), receiver (center) and cutter (forward) is paramount in the backdoor move. We use the guard's second or off hand as the key to the movement. As the guard's second hand comes to the ball indicating the pick up of the ball, the center comes to the elbow of the foul circle and the forward comes to the forward or wing receiving area. As the ball is passed to the center, the forward quickly reverses his direction and goes to the baseline and the basket. The center delivers a bounce pass to the cutting forward in the basket area.

The main purpose of the center and forward vacating the basket area together is to decrease the possibility of the defensive center clogging the area. Spacing is very important in any two- or three-player offensive movement.

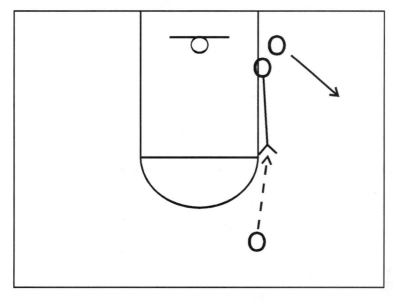

A. Center proceeds to elbow
B. Forward cuts to wing receiving area

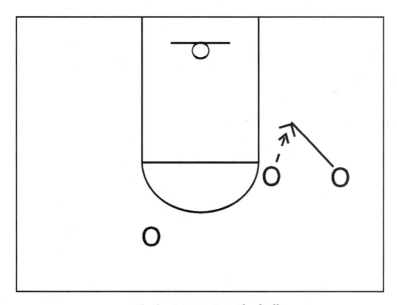

C. Center receives the ball
D. Forward reverses direction —
cuts to the basket and receives a bounce pass from the center

POST PLAY DEFENSE

Because of the differences in rules between amateur basketball and the NBA version, the defense of the post player at the two levels poses two different sets of problems. The NBA's no-zone rules impose distance limits for the defensive player. For example, the weakside defenders cannot leave their assigned players taking away a great deal of the backside help that a defensive post player needs to effectively contain the offensive opponent. In college and high school, there are no limits, and the weakside low defensive player can help his post teammate. To be effective, NBA defenders have come to rely on the double-team to contain the post player.

I will describe the various defensive positions of the post player. The post player's position will take away an opponent's offensive strength, but will also be exposed to the whatever countermove the offensive player executes after reading and reacting to the defense.

1. POST-UP PLAYER DEFENDED ON THE HIGH SIDE

This is a popular defensive position with many coaches because it reduces the chances of the defensive post player being sealed or screened if the pass from the wing player goes to the weakside forward at the free-throw line. This defensive position can pose problems for the offense, eliminating a seal position for the top-of-the-key pass. The offensive post player, however, can create a seal position on a highside post player should the wing player with the ball improve the passing angle to the post player with a dribble toward the baseline. Normally, this passing angle from the wing position is not a real option for the offensive post player as it must be passed toward the baseline midway between the backboard and the sideline. Because the post-up player is moving slightly away from the basket to receive the ball, the defensive post player can readjust the position between the basket and the offensive player receiving the pass.

This defensive position greatly reduces the chances of being sealed off from an inside pass toward the basket by the weakside forward who has flashed to the foul line area. By the same token, this highside position is vulnerable to the improved passing lane the wing player establishes by a dribble toward the baseline.

2. FRONTING THE POST PLAYER

Fronting the post player is a basic position many coaches use to prevent a strong scoring center from dominating the game. The old theory of not being able to score if you don't have the ball is the basis of this defense.

This type of post defense is helpful when seeing whether or not the offense can execute the lob pass to the inside. The lob pass tests players' peripheral vision, communication and quick reaction. Defensively, it's very important that the fronting defensive player use an aggressive and forcing defensive style against the passer as well as be able to rely on backside help. The defense on the passer is more important, however. A soft defense creates more problems for the fronting defensive player than a lack of backside help.

It is important to realize that the fronting defensive post player is in a poor rebounding position in the event of an outside shot. In most cases, the offensive post player is in position to easily screen out the defensive player. A coach who believes in a fronting defense may also want to use zone rebounding tactics. The fronting post player rebounds at the foul line and the two backline defensive players are positioned at each side of the basket to form a triangle of rebounders. If the offensive post-up player is an exceptional offensive rebounder, the weakside guard can go to the basket area to block out the offensive post player. I have seen other defensive guards come to a position at the top of the circle, positioned to go either way in the event of a long rebound.

Fronting the post player can be very effective if the total defensive rebounding plan is carried out and strong defensive pressure is put on the ball.

3. POST-UP PLAYER DEFENDED ON THE BASELINE OR LOW SIDE

This position has long been regarded as a fundamental side of the defensive postman with the ball at the wing or foul line extended. It forces the wing pass to an area where, conceivably, the defensive post player has help from the frontline defensive player who has retreated to the line of the ball which is at the wing. The frontline falloff, or slough, narrows the passing area from wing to post player in the defensive post, plays high on the side and discourages a routine pass to the shoulder of the receiver and on the opposite side of the defensive player.

With this lowside position, the defensive post man is in a good screening position in the event of an outside shot. If the ball is passed from the wing to the strongside guard, he should roll over the top and maintain a position toward the middle. Again, a highside contesting defensive position will force any pass to be angled toward the sideline, away from the basket. The strongside defensive forward, by a slight falloff of the opponent, will narrow the passing lane from the outside guard to the post-up player. Team help is absolutely vital to successful defensive post play.

If the defensive post players fail to roll over the top to the inside position as described above, they are vulnerable to a seal by the offensive post player and cannot prevent a pass into the paint area by an outside guard or a weakside forward flashing to the top of the circle and passing inside to the post player.

4. PLAYING BEHIND THE POST MAN

This is usually the least accepted defensive post position, but in certain circumstances it can be effective.

In the NBA many teams concede the inside post pass as part of a total defensive scheme. Coaches have given much thought to defending the post position. The preponderance of great scorers, both young and old, has created a change of defensive post policy. Prior to the hand-check rule, the 24-second clock was an integral part of game planning as it pertained to talented NBA centers. The hand check in the backcourt increased the amount of time the offense needed to get the ball past the midcourt line. Pressure on the ball and denial of a wing pass created more time problems for a team trying to get into its half-court offensive spacing. Often, only seven or eight seconds remained when the ball was being passed inside. It was almost invited inside by the defense which would almost immediately double-team the ballhandling center. The defensive post player took away the baseline by the overplay and the double-teaming weakside guard or forward took away a move toward the paint and basket. The result was a pass back out to the perimeter with little or no time for a return pass inside to the post player. The play took the ball out of the hands of the high-scoring center within 6 feet of the basket and put it into the hands of an outside shooter 20 feet from the basket.

Although the hand-check rule was reapplied in the 1970s, it gradually became an accepted defensive strategy until 1994 when it was ruled that the position and use of a legal forearm to prevent an offensive player from forcing his position was allowable without the impediment of a hand check. The philosophy of defensive play used by many coaches was based on the

24-second clock as an ally of their defense. This has been altered some-what by the latest rule changes, but coaches and players have always been able to adjust to the rules of the game as they learn through competition and experience.

The sum of what I have stated on this behind the post-up player is that it can be effective if a coach is willing to double-team the post-up player. It's a good defensive concept if the opponent's outside shooting is weak. This defensive position ensures good defensive screening.

Also, defending behind the post is good if the defense has an active, shot-blocking center. Playing behind the player is often intimidating and puts the defense in a position to block what is on each side of the basket and in the paint.

The basic weakness of playing directly behind a low post-up player, however, is a vulnerability to fouls. In most instances, a clever post-up player can create a foul situation by quick moves, pump fakes and power moves to the basket. A player who can shoot a sweeping hook shot can often get his in-close shot over the outstretched hand of the defensive post player who allows entry to the low post-up offensive player.

In the event of a double-team, the post-up player must make his offen-sive move quickly before the second defensive player doubles the ball. If the offensive player hesitates and allows the double-team, the low defen-sive player should cut off the baseline and the players in the double-team will close off the move to the paint area. This leaves a turnaround jump shot or the usual response of the low post offensive player, but the over-play to the baseline creates a problem for the hook shot toward the baseline.

RULES FOR DEFENSIVE POST PLAYERS

1. In a transition adjustment, try to beat the offensive post-up player to the player's favorite spot to set up post position. If he likes a medium low post, defensively occupy that position before the player gets back to the basket area. Make the offensive center go to the low post or high post.

2. The use of foot movements is very important. A defensive post-up player should be ACTIVE and adjust his position as the ball moves.

3. A post-up defensive player should communicate the exact position of his opponent. He should vocally yell the position — "low," "medium" or "high." If the ball is on the wing, it is important that defensive players playing the ball on the wing know what is behind them. If the post is low, there is less chance of the opponent driving to the baseline or cutting to the baseline after a pass inside to the post-up player. A cut over the top is a large defensive problem so an overplay to the dribble should be employed by the defensive wing player. Conversely, if the post is higher, the defensive

wing player is much more vulnerable to a baseline drive or a post pass and cut to the baseline. Again, help from the defensive post man will enable the defensive wing player to overplay his opponent to the baseline.

4. A defensive post player should contest the path of his opponent. Never allow the post-up player to move directly to a position on the strong side without some type of impediment.

5. A quick-moving defensive post player can confuse the offensive post-up player and the passer by varying the position of the post play. Circling can often discourage an inside pass or a soft inside passer can often be deluded into thinking the pass will reach the post-up player because the defensive player appears to be low-siding the post-up player. In reality, the defensive player is anticipating the soft pass and is willing to gamble on an interception. Alertness, anticipation and aggressiveness are mental requisites for sound individual defensive play. This is especially true in post play.

6. A good defensive post player should never lose sight of the ball. Midpoint is preferable. To maintain proper vision, move slightly back and away when the ball is on one side and the opponent is on the opposite side. Never trail the post-up player as the player comes to the ball side. Try to beat the opponent to the position the post-up player is trying to reach. Try to never concede a low post or medium post. Over-contesting a high post can result in a backcut and easy basket for the opponent.

7. The most important rule of all for a post defensive player is proper stance, vision and mental requirement. Stay low in a flexed-knee position, arms extended parallel to the floor, midpoint vision on the weak side, and anticipating movement of the opponent.

THE POSITIONS OF POST DEFENSE CIRCLING THE POST

1: 3/4 hand in lane denial

2: 3/4 deny position until pass is made to wing

3: ball on wing; post defense slip fronts

In 1 and 2, the ball is at the top and the post defender is in a three-quarters chest to shoulder denial position. The defender does not overstep his front foot to his opponent's less he get sealed for a reverse turn/seal and lob pass. It is important to have the arm denial in the passing lane area for deflection, not lunging for the post pass.

In the second and third photos, the top guard has passed the ball to the wing and the post defender corrects his position by slip fronting the offensive center. The post defender initiates the move by taking his left arm and raising it over the top of his opponent's right shoulder, keeping the left (or right) arm extended high to deter the post pass over the top. For the slip front to be effective, there has to be aggressive pressure on the ball outside and the post player must always keep a hand up to discourage a direct pass to the offensive center.

4: ball in corner; defense 3/4 deny hand in lane denial

In 4, the wing player recognizes that there is no clear passing angle and decides to dribble down the sideline to the baseline and try to make another entry to the post. The post defender takes his right foot and drops it behind the baseline foot to initiate another three-quarters denial defense. This position requires the defender to lean his chest against the shoulder of his opponent with the left arm extended into the passing lane of the center.

STRAIGHT UP POST DEFENSE FROM BEHIND

1   **2**

This defensive position demonstrates a flex arm in the back (1) with an outstretched hand on the low side. The post defender's footwork eliminates the baseline drop step power move (2). By tracing the ball fake made by the offensive player (2), we see the counter move for the offensive center is to try and go in the opposite direction (3).

3

All the while the post defender never loses his flex knee position (leverage) and holds defensive position until the help defense comes down or the opponent is forced to take an off-balance jump shot. Keep in mind that tracing the ball with one hand and keeping a flexed knee position with a flexed elbow to the back of the opponent is paramount to your success in this defensive position.

DRILLS FOR SKILLS

Because the center is usually the largest player on a team and plays in a defined area of the court, it is often assumed that his or her footwork is not as important as that of the smaller, moving guards and forwards. Actually, the reverse is true. The center is often called to make quick movements both on and off the ball.

THE JUMP STOP

Foot control is important at every position in basketball and possibly more important at the center position. The post player is usually situated, with or without the ball, in the center of the opponent's defense. It is important that the post player have the ability to move in any direction that presents a possible shot opportunity or away from double-team pressure. The jump stop is essential for any post player whose abilities are to be fully expressed.

The principle asset of the jump stop is that it enables the post player to use either foot as the pivot foot. This simply means the player can move in either direction. The stride stop determines the pivot foot as the ball is received limiting directional movement. The defensive player playing the post player can be more aggressive if the center is limited to only one direction on a reverse move, fake or a step-off move.

The jump stop is executed by a crow-hop type movement as the post receives the ball with both feet landing simultaneously on the floor. Either foot can be determined as the pivot foot. The position and pressure of the defensive post player then determines the pivot foot. A rule of thumb is that the pressure side of the post player determines that side as the pivot foot.

COACH/CENTER DRILL FOR DEVELOPING LOW BASE AND STANCE

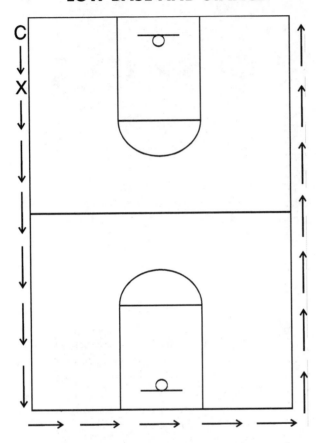

The coach (X) walks backward facing the center (C). The center, in a low stance, advances toward the coach. The coach passes the ball high or low to one side or the other; he can drop the ball, roll the ball or pass it quickly at the center's feet. The coach continues to walk backward in the direction of the arrows as the center catches the ball. The center must bring the ball to a low post stance with the ball at chest level. The drill continues as the coach and player work around the outside of the court as indicated by the directional arrows.

Important points to remember:
1. *The player must bring the ball to a flexed-knee position with the ball extended from the body whether the ball is a high or low pass.*
2. *The coach must vary the pass so the player learns to develop a wider area of pass reception.*
3. *The player must stay low the entire trip around the court.*
4. *The coach must conduct this drill outside of the sidelines and baselines either before or after practice.*
5. *Remember: this is a progressive development drill. Both parties must be patient with the center's progress. Coaches must be positive about the player's effort.*

JUMP STOP

1

2

In the first photo, the post player comes to a jump stop when going up for a post pass in the middle of the paint area. The second photo illustrates catching a pass with a jump stop with the feet parallel and no foot established as the pivot foot so that he can read and react. The last photo illustrates a jump stop with both feet parallel and the post player preparing for a reverse pivot or face-up, square-up shot attempt with the inside pivot foot.

3

CATCH AND SQUARE-UP
(ALSO KNOWN AS THE READ AND REACT BY A POST PLAYER)

The offensive center releases diagonally from the midpost to the middle of the free-throw line (see diagrams). His feet are parallel to the passer (1) as he sees the pass into his hands. The offensive center has a solid, balanced and wide base with his footwork as he keeps the ball chest high in the triple-threat position (1, 2). He reads his defender (2) and protects the ball against an attempt to reach in by the defense. In all of the photos, the offensive center is able to use any and all necessary one-on-one moves when attacking the basket offensively. Observe that the offensive center pictured does not predetermine his footwork or next move when he patiently reads the defense. He can drop-step (reverse pivot) or front turn. Because the defense is loose and cannot block the shot attempt, the receiver squares up and goes into a shooting motion (3).

PIVOT DRILLS: FRONT PIVOT AND REAR PIVOT

One of the first definite descriptions of a basketball player was that of the post or center: the "pivot player." The pivot was and still is an important part of effective post play. The pivot is best employed from a low flexed-knee position. The hips are a swivel that often can control and neutralize the defensive post player by sealing or screening him away from the ball. It is also effectively used when the defense takes a high overplay to discourage a pass into the post. A reverse pivot can allow the post player to seal the defensive player on the opposite side of his defensive position. This reverse pivot is a seldom-used part of post play yet is an integral maneuver if the post player is to effectively seal or screen an opponent in the two-player game. A tight screen by the post player will often necessitate a defensive switch enabling the post player to create a seal position on the player screened. A reverse pivot will cause the defensive player to lose position on the post player who has screened inside.

One of the most effective and popular post moves in basketball today is the front pivot. It is necessary for an effective front pivot spin move that is a response to an aggressive defensive post player who is physically leaning and pushing the offensive post player. It's not effective against a soft defender in most instances.

Simple, basic pivot drills were part of most daily practice sessions. The drills would stress: a) the jump stop and b) the pivot with either the right foot or left foot established as the pivot foot. Situations would be created that would arise in game type situations to create the proper physical response needed for the situation. An example would be the pivot used by the screen in center-forward play: two-player screen at the wing position as opposed to a pivot used by a post player to establish a post position.

The following diagrams should show this difference in the pivot used in two-player drills — post pivots.

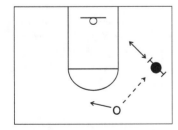 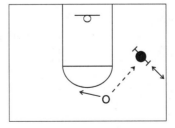 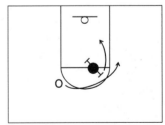

Inside foot as the pivot foot   *Outside foot as the pivot foot*   *Inside pivot with the ball*

PROBLEMS WHEN USING THE OUTSIDE FOOT AS THE PIVOT FOOT

When the wing players use the outside foot as the pivot foot, they encounter the following problems:

- Using the outside foot as the pivot foot (the foot closest to the sideline) to face-up to the basket creates a front turn. A front turn exposes the back to an alert, aggressive defensive player and can cause a turnover.

- If the outside foot becomes the pivot foot, the ability to counter the defense with a reverse turn is lost. A spin move can be used, but is usually not effective this far from the basket.

- In the diagrams on the preceding page, the arrow shows the 3 to 4 feet of distance lost when using the outside foot as the pivot foot. The direction of the inside foot is toward the middle of the court as it faces up with the pivot foot.

THE DEVELOPMENT OF INDIVIDUAL FOOT SKILLS

Basketball is a game of countermoves. Each foot skill counters a defensive play.

EXPLOSION STEP

This is particularly effective when using the two-player screen. As one player comes to set a screen, the player with the ball should fake in the opposite direction. This causes the defensive player to make a decision — whether to go over or under the screen — which divides the attention of the defense. As the ball handler steps off with the faking foot and comes around the screener, the defensive player is totally concerned with getting around or under the screen. The ball handler sets up the defensive player by stepping off and coming over the screen. Now the ball handler steps off and explodes to the basket off the step-off foot.

Also effective in a straight one-on-one situation, it's best used after the offensive player has foot faked his direction of movement. The move is best executed by a moderate speed foot fake with an explosion of the step-off foot. The move should always be set up. This move can be implemented into a daily 15-minute practice drill before, during or after practice so players become more familiar with their teammates' footskills and offensive moves to the basket.

EXPLOSION STEP

1   **2**

The defensive center is caught flat-footed by the aggressive explosion step that is executed by the offensive center (1). The offensive center takes one dribble to finish the move to the basket (2).

SPIN MOVE

The spin move is gaining much popularity. It is one of the few moves effectively using the front pivot in the modern game. Although it's more effective from a short post position, it can also be used to counter an overly aggressive defender whose momentum often has him moving toward the sideline. The offensive player uses a dribble to execute a front turn and spin away from the defender. The dribble should not begin until the spin move has been completed. Basics of the spin move follow:

1. It can be employed to the right or left but is most effective when spinning toward the baseline.

2. The post player executes a front pivot — a pivot away from the defender — dribbling only after completing the turn to the baseline.

3. The defender is aggressively bodying or physically hand-checking the post player. As the post player executes the front turn to the basket, the momentum of the defender is toward the sideline — the direction opposite the basket. Because it is a front turn, the defender ends up "pushing air" and the post player proceeds to the basket.

4. It can be used against a loose defender or a defender who pushes and then falls back.The counter is the front turn with the lead foot crossing over from its original plant position near the baseline to a crossover step toward the paint area. As this crossover step is made,the ball should be swung very low to the floor and a short dribble into the paint area with a hook shot developing. When used with a front turn with the lead foot planted in the base area and crossed over to the baseline area, a power move off this same short dribble can effectively be used.

Photos illustrating the footskills used in the spin move are found in chapter five, page 37. I would encourage you to turn there if you have any questions regarding the techniques described above.

REVERSE DRIVE

This is a very basic but very important move for any basketball player to master. Its primary use is to counter an aggressive, denying defensive player who has a tendency to overextend his defense. The inside foot must be the pivot foot. The reverse turn must have the step-off foot pointed toward the basket and the ball should not be dribbled toward the sideline but in the same direction as the step-off foot.

In many ways, this can be the most important move a player can master. It creates a threat to drive to the basket, as it (1) causes the defensive player to reverse positions, (2) forces the defense to react to the motion and (3) allows the offensive player to finish the play with a drive or come back to a normal face-up position with excellent spacing between the offensive player and the defensive matchup.

Basketball, unlike most team sports, can be practiced by individuals, independent of coaching or teaching. Foot skills, dribbling and shooting are just examples of how a player can take his or her game to a higher level by simply making a commitment of time and effort to perfecting these skills. The same skills that can elevate a guard's effectiveness are the same skills a center can refine to raise his game to a higher level.

ROCKER STEP

This is a countermove off a foot fake by the offensive player to drive the opponent back and create more space between the offensive player and the opponent. The mechanics of the move are a step-off by the offensive player who is playing low with flexed knees creating an impression of foot faking and coming back to a normal face-up position. The extended foot keeps its position and the fake is an upper torso fake — from the hips to the head — with the knees staying in a flexed position. The head fake back is an important part of the total fake and it often causes the defensive player to move toward the offensive player. Since the knees are in their original flexed position, the offensive player is in a physical position which allows a quick drive to the basket as the defensive player's motion is toward the offensive player. Once this happens, it's very difficult for the defense to pick up the drive. This is a fine countermove to an aggressive defensive player who is susceptible to any fake.

OFFENSIVE REBOUNDING ILLUSTRATIONS

While defensive rebounding is technique, offensive rebounding is more cerebral — anticipation, mental and physical aggressiveness, use of leg strength, and real desire for the ball.

An offensive rebounder, other than the shooter, should expect the shot to miss and anticipate where the ball will go. Some offensive rebounders are often inactive until they see the shot has missed, making them easy targets for screening because their response to the missed shot came too late.

As the ball is in flight, the offensive rebounder should be maneuvering the opponent by faking direction of movement. A fake in one direction can cause the defensive rebounder to respond in that direction and can set up the use of a reverse pivot that will screen the defensive rebounder from a rebound. The smaller players are often the greatest offensive rebounders because their constant movements create real problems for the defense. Two outstanding rebounders who could barely dunk the ball — Charles Oakley and Paul Silas — depended on their foot skills to position themselves for the rebound. Both were adept at circling the opponent, proceeding to the baseline, and establishing a position under the basket and moving the defensive rebounder, who is now behind them, away from the basket area. They have caused a reverse of positions by this movement.

The term "garbage player" describes players who always seem to come up with the easy rebounds and loose balls in the basket area. These players are active, scoring players who anticipate and are alert. I am not sure that it can be taught, but I do know it is intuitive with these types of players.

LOW POST OFFENSIVE REBOUNDING POSITION

The medium post player is defended with a 3/4 denial (1), the offensive post player recognizes that a perimeter shot is about to be taken (2) and begins the footwork to pivot around the 3/4 denial defense (3). (Action sequence continues on facing page.)

LOW POST OFFENSIVE REBOUNDING POSITION (CONTINUED)

5

6

The offensive post player seals the inside position (4, 5, 6) for a ready rebound position if there is a missed attempt. Notice that the offensive player never uses his hands to keep the defender behind him once the offensive player has secured the inside position. The offenisve player's arms are extended and his hands are ready for the put back shot. This is an extremely important aspect of proper offensive rebounding position.

7

OFFENSIVE REBOUNDING FOOTWORK

1

2

The shot is taken from the perimeter and the defensive center screens or blocks out the offensive center (1). The shot is released (2). (Action sequence continues on facing page.)

OFFENSIVE REBOUNDING FOOTWORK (CONTINUED)

3

4

The offensive center takes his right foot and steps around the blockout for inside position (3). This offers the opportunity for a rebound of his teammate's missed shot (4).

OFFENSIVE REBOUNDING SIDE VIEW OF THE WEAKSIDE POST

1

2

3

4

The defensive center has flex elbow contact on the weakside center (1). The weakside offensive center recognizes his teammate's shot attempt and takes his right foot to step around the defensive center (2). The shot releases (3) and the offensive center has the inside position for any missed shot attempt as the opposing defensive center has lost the rebounding position and advantage (4).

Observe the sequence of offensive rebounding footskills that are necessary in becoming an effective offensive rebounder.

THE HANDS UP DRILL

The proper stance for a basketball player, regardless of position, is a
flexed-knee stance with the arm up and away from the body. All movement originates from a flexed-knee position. If a player is standing straight-
legged, an opponent in a flexed-knee position has a decided advantage in
any movement. The straight-legged player is not ready to move until the
knees are bent putting the player one motion behind.

The flexed-knee position is particularly important for the center or post
player. Not only is the center ready to move and receive the ball from a
teammate, but the physical base is lower presenting more of a problem for
the defensive player. This low base allows the post player to be able to
physically maintain position when encountering defensive pushing from
the rear. They will also be in better control of the defensive player with the
swivel of the hips as the defense tries to circle and to crow-hop to meet the
ball as it proceeds toward the player.

Along with flexing the knees, the correct position of the arms also is
important. They should be up and away at all times for all players, particularly for a center or post player. When the arms are extended the players
have a better sense of balance and create more of a problem for defensive
post players because they impede the movement of the defensive players
in their effort to deflect or intercept entry passes. Further, proper extension of the arms puts offensive players in a position to receive the ball.
With the arms at the side, receiving players often resist the ball as their
hands are moving toward the intended pass which creates a fumbled pass
in most instances.

Standing upright with the arms alongside and downward are normal physical acts. This lessens a basketball player's capability for good, effective
play, however. Neither words nor vocal exhortations will have any mean-
ing unless the player is conditioned in the proper physical stance. I have
found the hands-up drill particularly effective for all basketball players but
especially for post players.

If used as a team drill, the players are dispersed over the lower third of
the court. They are instructed to have one foot forward, the other backward in a comfortable defensive stance. The hands are to be in a defensive
position. If the right foot is forward, the right hand is up as if in the face of
the opponent. The left arm and hand are about hip level, parallel to the
floor. The coach dispenses the players throughout the area in several rows
about 6 feet laterally and 6 feet in the rows. A smaller court may require
more rows and less space between players. The coach gives four direc-

tions of movement — forward, rear, right and left. The cadence should vary. Rapid changes of directions often quicken player responses. The coach will get the feel for the changes as he or she feels more comfortable with the drill.

I believe strongly in vocally conducting the drill. Some coaches prefer pointing the arms to indicate change of direction. Because the arms soon become leaden and start to drop, the vocal conduct of the drill can be more demanding in keeping the arms up. Again, the coach is conditioning the players to properly move and operate in the correct stance. The knees begin to stiffen and the arms begin to drop as the players get tired. The coach must vocally implore the players to stay with knees flexed and hands up.

I cannot totally relate the many benefits this drill gives a coach and team. Not only does it develop proper body and arm positions, but the players learn to "suck it up." They will want to drop their hands and stand straight up in a normal position because they are enduring physical pain, especially in their arms. But they learn to fight through pain and endure it. How often do we see players lessen their speed and movement in transition defense because they are tired and it is easier to let someone else pick up their player? This drill will create a habit of fighting through this thought of letting up. It creates a mutual respect of the players for each other as they know their teammates have also hung in when the desire to quit was strong.

This drill should be exercised early in the season from a team standpoint. Because the drill demands muscle use in the calves, upper legs, and arm support to maintain both the flexed-knee position and the arms up and away, it's not necessarily a good drill throughout the year. For high school players, I recommend it initially be used for a two-minute period without a stop. One minute right foot forward, one minute left foot forward. Each day add one minute and divide the time with each foot forward. I would not exceed 12 minutes without stopping for high school players. I ran it for 20 minutes with my college teams and started with three minutes and added two minutes each day until I reached 12 minutes. I then added one minute.

This drill also develops foot ambidexterity, something sadly lacking in teaching many players today. Because the position of the foot changes, the demand of each foot changes. As a center drill alone, the individual can be taken to an unused portion of the court with his assistant coach conducting the same hands-up drill that was just described. The constant, repetitious demand of the low stance and extended arms will build muscle support that will enable the player to hold the fundamental lateral movement and quickness that is so important in center play.

THE HANDS UP DRILL

Review the diagram of this drill first, then observe how we have spaced the players apart and the defensive positions they assume for the drill. The first photo demonstrates the players with the left foot forward, left arms extended above their heads and the right hands down and away from their bodies. They are ready for the coach's command to shuffle forward toward half-court. The same is true in the second photo, but the opposite hand is up. The same command follows.

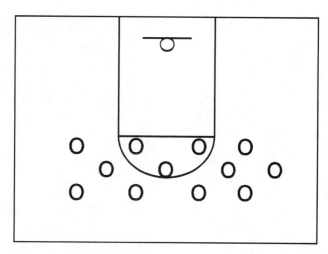

1

2

HANDS UP DRILL (CONTINUED)

Side view of correct defensive position for hands up drill for team and/or center forwards. Notice in all the pictures that the hands are extended high for a shot, the knees are flexed, and the opposite hand is ready to defend the pass.

Finally, this drill creates muscle support for the legs and arms. The arms often drop because there is not enough upper arm muscle support to keep the hands in their proper upright position. The legs stiffen so they can rely on the knee to support the body because the calf and upper leg muscle supports need strengthening. The hands-up drill will develop the physical strength to maintain the accepted fundamental position of a basketball player.

DEFENSIVE REBOUNDING

Although it is definitely an asset, leaping ability isn't all that is necessary for defensive rebounding. Too often the leaper relies only on this natural talent and does not perform the important function because of poor technique. There are various schools of thought on the proper procedures to execute this important skill. Regardless of the different approaches, the most important part of defensive rebounding is the angle of the defensive rebounder who leaps for the ball.

To me, defensive rebounding is about technique — proper technique. Important in this technique is the low base of the defensive rebounder. The low base insures a real resistance to a push by his offensive opponent, creates contact and a control of the opponent's movement. This low base should be established as the ball is first in the air. The arms should be up and extended with the hands above the shoulder and upper arms lateral to the floor. The arm and hand position gives the post player better balance and added control of the offensive rebounder being screened.

This physical contact should be maintained and the offensive rebounders controlled physically as they try to work around the defensive rebounder or physically force the defensive rebounder to a position under the basket. Sometimes a defensive rebounder must attempt to move his opponent away from the basket area if both players are in a close-to-the-basket vicinity so a slight movement backward will be necessary. It is very difficult to jump from a stiff-knee position, and the backward movement of the defensive rebounder helps keep the offensive rebounder from effectively jumping.

The angle of the body of the defensive rebounder is extremely important. It can best be described as a 45-degree angle when the defensive rebounder leaps for the ball. This angle ensures reception of the ball. The only way the opposing rebounder can possibly get the ball is by fouling over the back of the rebounder.

The initial low base of the defensive rebounder allows the proper angle. Furthermore, the range of rebound recovery is greater. Both the proper angle and range, and rebound recovery are essential elements of defensive technique and rebounding. A defensive rebounder must never move toward the basket until he has established contact.

DEFENSIVE BLOCKOUT/REBOUNDING DRILL

This drill is very important to implement into your daily pre-season drills. This combination drill can be continued throughout the regular season at least once a week, depending on your order of the team's needs for fundamental drills. One of the principle elements of a solid defensive team is the ability of your team to always blockout and anticipate every opponent's missed field goal attempt.

If you, as a coach, predetermine that your team is small and doesn't possess the leaping ability to contend versus taller more athletically inclined opponents, then you have conceded an important variable in all of basketball coaching: teaching. If you instruct your players early in the preseason about this important aspect of the team philosophy, you're more than likely to capture your team's commitment to this area of team defense. Thus, you have the necessary mental preparation and attention already presented and ready for instruction. This drill is a team drill and all participants and backups should be verbal, supportive of the teammates' efforts to come up with the missed shot. Remember that you should not allow your players to slack from the normal team defensive rules.

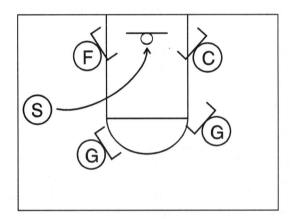

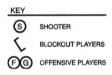

Rules:
Players pass and cut out of normal sets.
1. Triangle situations
2. Motion/flex offense
3. Pick and rolls
4. Call screens, switch, help on drives
5. Players must maintain vision of the ball at all times
6. The coach will always take missed shots
7. The players must rebound/outlet to guards on the sideline
8. The approximate time of the drill should be 12 minutes.
9. The coach is to move from side to top to side and the guards must always make themselves available for outlet passes after rebounds.
10. The defense stays on the court until the rebound is gathered.
11. The play moves from offense to defense.
12. The inactive players are to stay at halfcourt not sidelines as rebounder might confuse receivers on an outlet pass.

DEFENSIVE REBOUNDING POSITION WEAKSIDE — SIDEVIEW

In this sequence of defensive positions by the post defender, observe that the offensive center is making his motion toward the ball (1 and 2). The defensive post player is denying the passing lane (1) and preparing to pivot off his left foot when going into his blockout motion as the shot is attempted from the opposite side of the court (2). Note the defensive player's use of his peripheral vision in photos 1 and 2 and the defensive player's flexed knees in the blockout position with arms in the ready rebound position (3 and 4).

DEFENSIVE REBOUND — OVER THE TOP VIEW

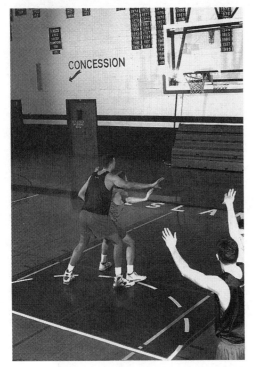

This camera angle illustrates the footwork necessary to properly block out on the shot attempt.

CONCLUSION

Basketball is a simple game, often defined as a game of simplicity and execution. It is a game that seldom demands more than three of its five players involved offensively — a screener, a cutter and a passer. Conversely, it is a game that demands all five of its players working as a unit to properly play defense. It is a game in which a single player can operate successfully on offense when isolated with the defensive player, yet one defensive player who doesn't play within the defensive scheme of the team can break down the team defense, which is required to rotate the other four players because of the defensive individualism of one player.

There is one constant that is evident in every phase of offense — man, switch, zone, against a press, delayed game and stall game — spacing. Basically spacing is the concept that attempts to isolate the defense from the point of attack — the eventual shot. Proper spacing enables the offense to counter the defense's attempt to double the ball or over extend itself to defend the point of attack. The theory has never been more evident than in the NBA with their various defensive double down tactics on the offensive post players and doubling the ball in the two-man game initiated often at the wing position. Spacing of the perimeter offensive people is an absolute must if the offense is to counter this extra pressure on the ball when it is inside.

When we think of the simplicity of the game, it is difficult to refute the adage that basketball is a game of habit and counters. Habits, be they good or bad, are the results of repetitious physical acts. A bad habit will prevail unless the coach, through constant, fundamentally correct drills, creates a good habit. The coach can only condition the good habit by physically repetitive drills. A proper habit will never be formed by chalk, vocal recriminations or any appeal other than the physical, repetitive appeal I have alluded to above.

To say basketball is a game of counters seems almost trite until the game and its tactics, strategy, methods of play, and adjustments that are often necessary — offensively and defensively — are taken into consideration. Team defenses that attempt to force the offense to play a tempo of game that is not their normal tempo, to take away the primary strength and depend on secondary alternative, that force an opponent to beat the defense from the strength of their perimeter game or allow the ball inside and shut off the perimeter game are but instances of the importance of counters.

A defensive player is often instructed to play his or her offensive player a certain way. It may be a tight, loose or overplay to the right or left. It is up to the offensive player to read the defensive position and respond by countering. The counter is to attack the defense at its weakest point — if it is a loose defense the shot is the counter; if it is a right or baseline overplay then a drive to the middle is the counter, a left overplay opens a drive baseline and a tight aggressive play demands a reverse drive, a spin move or a fake reverse drive and face up after the defensive player has been forced to retreat by the deep reverse foot action. Simply, it is called the read and react theory. Read the defense and react to what is being given to the offensive player. The above pertains to a face up player in the vicinity of the wing position.

The same theory of read and react is a major part of successful offensive play for the center or post player. There are many more reads for the center than there are at the wing position. The post player has the double team, the three-second area, and potential cutters to the basket that demand attention and a possible pass. He or she must also deal with a congested area with extra hands slapping at the ball. Their decisions must be almost of an intuitive nature. It is a very difficult position to play with decisions that are determined by the various defensive reactions. How does the coach address the problems of the proper response?

Part-method teaching allows for the teacher to break down the offensive sets into component parts called part-method drills. Part-method teaching creates the many recognition factors the offensive players must read and respond to. The passer must read the position of the screener and the path of the cutter. If the defense switches, the open player will most probably be the screener. If it's a man-to-man defense, the cutter will usually be the open player. This is but an example of the read and react concept. The concept can only be taught through repetitious drills. As an individual offensive player reacts to what the defense is taking away and what is being given and reads the defensive strategy as taught through the part-method teaching, the counter will often be successfully employed.

I have found that players — men and women — at all levels of competition react favorably to teaching. By creating drills that increase their understanding of the game and recognize the intellectual response as well as the physical response, players seldom reject this theory. Basketball has been over-coached and under-taught for the last several decades but it appears that it is slowly reverting back to the teaching importance in the individual and team development.

To me coaching and teaching are not the same. Coaching refers to the five player aspects of the game — type or style of offense and defense, tactics, strategy, daily practice plan, leadership, discipline, psychological preparations, bench coaching and other such matters that pertain to the teams as a whole. Teaching is the individual attention given to the players as it applies to the development and refinement of their skills, the various techniques — screening, rebounding, defensive fundamentals of play and the offensive elements of passing, dribbling, shooting and footwork skills that have been described in earlier chapters. It is important that the head coach objectively assesses his strengths and weaknesses and attempts to form a staff that has skills that complement his.

What we have attempted to do in this book is to reacquaint the coach with the historical background and development of the post player from the earliest day until the present day. To see how the center players have caused radical rule changes and how their latest input has been lessened by these same rules committees. Basketball has always been a game of change that is caused by differing interpretations of rules and changes in the rules themselves. Any rule change should be closely studied by every coach to see how that new rule can prove to be a benefit to his or her style of play, not a detriment. Regardless of a personal dislike of a new rule, a coach must accept it and try to make it work for him or her.

We have devoted much of our teaching to the counter theory. It is important that a basketball player not pre-suppose situations but read them before responding. If the coach can prevail upon the player that while it is important to read and recognize what the defense is taking away and allowing, it is even more important that the player gives his or her game the dimensions of play that allow the offensive player to attack the defensive position. If the defense overplays the right side, it is important that the offensive player can drive off the left side to defeat the overplay. There is a counter for every defensive overplay, but to develop the counter demands much work and repetition by the player and much patience and encouragement by the coach.

ABOUT THE AUTHORS

Pete Newell is a consultant and west coast scout with the Cleveland Cavaliers. His contributions to basketball span over 50 years. Newell has guided teams to both NCAA (California-Berkeley, 1959) and NIT Championships (San Francisco, 1949), directed the United States men's basketball team to a gold medal in the 1960 Olympics, was named College Coach-of-the-Year (1960) and won the highly coveted Metropolitan Award — given annually by college coaches to the man who has contributed the most to the game of basketball.

Over the past 15 years, Tom Newell has established himself as one of the NBA's top assistant coaches. He was coached with the Dallas Mavericks, New Jersey Nets, Seattle Supersonics, Indiana Pacers, and Golden State Warriors. He is also president of Family First Productions.